# 101 Commonsense Rules for the Office

## *How to Get Along and Get Ahead*

### John R. Brinkerhoff

STACKPOLE
BOOKS

Published by
STACKPOLE BOOKS
Cameron and Kelker Streets
P.O. Box 1831
Harrisburg, PA 17105

*Illustrations by Durf McJoynt*
*Cover design by Tracy Patterson*

Printed in the United States of America

First Edition

10 9 8 7 6 5 4 3 2

**Library of Congress Cataloging-in-Publication Data**

Brinkerhoff, John R.
    101 commonsense rules for the office / John R. Brinkerhoff.
        p.    cm.
    ISBN 0-8117-2418-2
    1. Career development.   2. White collar workers.   3. Office politics.   4. Business etiquette.   I. Title.
    HF5381.B653    1992
    651′.023′73—dc20                                    91-27344
                                                        CIP

# Contents

# Socializing at the Office . . . . . . . . . . . . . . . 68

# How to Get Ahead . . . . . . . . . . . . . . . . . . . 86

# Supervising . . . . . . . . . . . . . . . . . . . . . . . . 97

# Office Ethics . . . . . . . . . . . . . . . . . . . . . . . 111

# Introduction

This is a rule book for office workers—anyone who is engaged primarily in transmitting information rather than in making some tangible device or providing a specific service. Office workers write papers, go to meetings, assemble and analyze data, and talk on the phone. They are employed by corporations, governments, universities, foundations, churches, and other large organizations. An organization is large when it is too big to function as one intimate group and has to be subdivided into several smaller groups or work centers in order to accomplish its mission. The necessity for these smaller groups to communicate among themselves brings into being the peculiar human behavior characteristic of large organizations. Many organizations with fewer than 100 employees—including law firms, professional medical corporations, colleges, real estate offices, and consulting companies—have the characteristics of large organizations.

Large organizations are necessary. An individual human being can accomplish little working alone. Humans working in groups can do things beyond the capability of the group members working individually. The larger the project, the larger the organization required to do the work. Large organizations have been required for the complex projects of civilization. Indeed, an ability to work together and coordinate the activities of small work groups to achieve goals beyond what an individual or a small work group could achieve separately may be the essence of civilization. Large organizations built the pyramids, established the Roman Empire, created merchant banking, explored the world, and reached the moon.

Americans have an intense love-hate relationship with large organizations. In the United States large organizations are unpopular with most people—even the people who work in them. Yet we also rely on them. We denigrate the U.S. Postal Service, but we count on the mail arriving. We complain about the U.S. Army, but we turn to its methods when we want to get a job done. We disparage large corporations, but we buy their products. We extol the virtues of the lone hero—farmer, gunfighter, or entrepreneur—but we do almost all of our work in large organizations. Indeed, the large organization appears to have been designed with the United States in mind. In a large nation with a large population, a large supply of resources, and a large economy, large organizations are necessary to plan and carry out large programs.

The effectiveness of a large organization depends on its employees—primarily the managers, but also the production workers, service providers, and to a great extent the office workers who integrate the work. No large organizations are perfect, and some are much better than others. Most large organizations operate well enough to survive. Some flourish; some fail. All have work environments with some common characteristics, and it is the degree of adaptability of the employees to the work environment that contributes a great deal to success or failure.

These rules are intended to help office workers understand and adapt to the work environment of large organizations. These are "commonsense" rules based primarily on my own experience as an office worker in large organizations. I am giving you my opinions, and you can judge as to whether they are helpful. I have tried to point up the ethical and moral questions facing office workers while also providing practical advice for day-to-day living. There could probably be more rules, but 101 seemed a sufficiently large number for both the author and the reader. I have grouped related rules into chapters, but each rule is designed to convey a whole thought.

The best time to read this book is on the bus going to work. Despite your eagerness, try to limit yourself to one rule per business day. Don't read it on the bus on the way home from work because you will be too tired to enjoy it then, and that is nap time anyway. If you drive, I advise you to resist the urge to read it while stuck in traffic during rush hour on the freeway. Carpoolers might persuade one of the group to read a rule aloud each morning. If you don't ride the bus or have a car pool, read it during your coffee breaks.

Good luck to you office workers. You are a much misunderstood and much maligned group. You are better than most people believe you to be, but you are not yet as good as you can be. These rules are designed to help you achieve your organizational potential.

# The Boss

Every book is supposed to have a beginning, a middle, and an end. I didn't have much trouble with the end, and the middle sort of fell into place, but the beginning was tough. Where do you start a list of rules for better office performance?

After a lot of thought, I decided to start with some rules for dealing with the boss. The boss is important in one's work life—perhaps the most important factor. This is true for all commercial, government, academic, for-profit and nonprofit organizations.

Another consideration is that everyone has a boss. No matter how high one gets, there is always a boss up there somewhere. In a large corporation it is possible to trace the boss line up until one reaches the acme of bosses—the chief executive officer. For the government that is the President of the United States. For private industry that is the chairman or president. However, even these highest ranking bosses have bosses. The President of the United States has a boss or many bosses—the people. The CEO of a corporation certainly has to answer to shareholders and possibly to customers. The president of a university has to answer to the faculty, the students, the alumni, the football coach, and so on.

Here are some rules on the care and feeding of bosses. This is necessary in a hierarchy and a bit risky, but it can be highly rewarding.

# Rule 1: Know Who Your Boss Is

One of the most important rules for success in the office is to know who your boss is. This may seem simple, but like other aspects of working in an office, it is not always easy.

The term "boss" can have different meanings.

1. **Your supervisor.** This is the person who gives you assignments, reviews your work, and rates you. The term is sometimes made even more explicit by adding the word "direct." Your direct supervisor often is your real boss as well, but not always.

2. **Your mentor.** Sometimes a person in the chain of command above you will help your career and give you valuable tips and contracts. This is your mentor. This is seldom your direct supervisor because a mentor usually is a very senior person, but a combination of the two is not unheard of.

3. **Your role model.** This usually is a person who inspires you and, in fact, is your real leader. This may be your supervisor; if so, you are lucky. It is likely to be your mentor, because we all tend to like those who are helping us, but it could be another person entirely. Quite often the role model is your supervisor's supervisor or someone higher up. However, it may be a senior person in another branch, division, directorate, or office.

4. **The real power.** Ever since sociologists found out about "informal organization," workers have looked to see who is really running things. This means that your supervisor may not be—is unlikely to be—the real power in your organization. The real power is the person who is really in charge, sets the agenda, and gets things done. It is often the person to whom the big boss looks for progress. The real power may or may not be your supervisor, but there always will be such a person.

Few office workers have mentors. Most have role models. Most will be connected in some way to real powers. All have supervisors. You will have to select one of these as your boss. It is highly unlikely that the same individual will play all of these roles. You may have to deal with two, three, or even four bosses, all of whom have some degree of influence over your work and career.

This will not be a problem until there is a conflict. Suppose you get an order from your supervisor that conflicts with an order from the real power. Whom do you obey? Suppose you get inspiration from your role model that irritates your supervisor. Whom do you please? Suppose your mentor holds principles that conflict with the ideals of your role model? Whom do you follow?

You can bet your bottom dollar that such conflicts will occur. Suppose that your supervisor tells you not to contact another agency on some legislation, but you meet the real power in the hallway and he says you should by all means contact that other agency. What do you do? Say your supervisor tells you to fax some data to a branch office right away, but the real power has put out the word that he wants to see everything that leaves the office first. You will have to decide who your real boss is on each of these occasions.

To survive, the answer is clear. Only one of these four people is required to grade your performance periodically and agree with proposed promotions, awards, bonuses, and transfers. That is your direct supervisor. Therefore, no matter how much you may want to follow the lead of these other bosses, the real boss is the person who rates you. This is the boss to whom you owe your primary loyalty.

## Rule 2: Make the Boss Look Good

One of the ways to get ahead is to make your boss look good. The idea is that you will look good if the boss looks good. That is not always true, since this depends on the kind of boss you have.

It will do no good to make some bosses look good. They expect you to make them look good and take it for granted when you do. So if you do your job in such a way as to really give a boost to the boss, it is quite possible that you will receive not only no thanks but no credit. On the other hand, it is highly dangerous to make such a boss look bad, even accidentally. It is critical to avoid such blunders.

If you have an average good boss, it can help a lot to make him or her look good. You can write his or her papers so that they sparkle. You can prepare his or her briefings or speeches to the luncheon club so he or she sounds like a brilliant orator. You can even praise the boss behind his or her back (pretty extreme stuff!). These things will make the boss look good. They will also make you look good.

Almost everyone in an office knows who does what and who does not. In particular, it is well understood who the "horses" are in each office—who really does the work. Those who just tag along are also well known. If your boss starts looking really good and excels, it will not be long before you are tagged as the reason. This will raise your standing with your peers and set a good climate for advancement. It will also give you a reputation for selflessness, in that you have gone all out to make your boss look good. That you are doing this out of a sense of self-enhancement rather than philanthropy for bosses will not be lost but will be submerged in the general climate of good will engendered by your actions.

If this all works out as expected, of course, making the boss look good will also make him or her grateful. You may be rewarded with pay increases, promotions, bonuses, and maybe even a cushy trip.

## Rule 3: Don't Surprise the Boss

Bosses do not like surprises. They like to know exactly what is going on and exactly what is going to happen next.

So you should never surprise the boss about work things. It is all right to throw a surprise birthday party or something like that; it is not all right to allow him or her to receive a call from an irate peer or, worse, the Big Boss, about a problem of which he or she has never heard. If the problem concerns you and something you have done or not done, then you are in big trouble. Rightfully so. If something happens, good or bad, the first person to tell is the boss.

It may seem elementary, but don't contradict the boss in public. That is a most unpleasant surprise for the boss. If you have changed your position, tell the boss about it even if you don't have to get his or her approval. The boss is likely to approve of what you want to do and will support you on an issue until you tell him or her that it should be changed. Never embarrass the boss before his or her peers.

I remember a conference I attended with a group of important people. One of my employees was on the program. I had not rehearsed the presentation because I trusted the employee and did not require "murder boards" before allowing my people to give briefings. Generally, that policy proved to be a good one. It saved time and built confidence. In this case it was a disaster. I had been informed by this employee that we were, say, in favor of blue widgets for a particular program. I had spoken up forcefully for blue widgets at previous meetings and at this one. Imagine my horror when my employee advocated red widgets during his briefing. I never heard the end of that. It made me look like a fool because it appeared as if I did not even know what color widgets we wanted. I was upset and let the offender know.

My advice is to keep the boss informed. Never surprise him or her with information that has changed. If you are in doubt, consult the boss. It is important in a large organization to maintain a united front within an office, department, or agency. You have to play your part in maintaining that unity. Keeping the boss informed is a good idea.

## Rule 4: Have a Document for the Boss

You know how it is. The boss calls or hurries into your office. He says, "I've got to brief the vice president for marketing on the Smith problem in thirty minutes. Give me what you've got on it."

As a good employee, you want to help the boss. You want to make him look smart and feel good. So you pull out the file on the Smith problem and refresh your memory. Although complicated, the issues are clear. You wonder how to pass this information to the boss so he can report to the vice president for marketing.

My advice is to do it in writing. You can go up to the boss's office and brief him orally, but always have a document for him to digest. If he hasn't time for you to brief him, he will at least be able to read the facts.

One of the problems with being a boss is that there is always more to do than can be done. Bosses have bosses and someone above is always wanting to know what is going on. So you should be good at providing succinct written reports to save time for you and your boss.

This is not intended to discourage informal talks, which remain important. It does suggest that there are many times that a short document is highly useful alone or to supplement an oral report.

The ability to compress information and still present the whole story clearly is learned, not inherited. Many people, unfortunately, do not know how to write a short information paper or fact sheet properly. One of the most important things is to put it all on one piece of paper. Bosses have little time to read and most don't like to read. They are far more likely to read a one-page note than a lengthy report. So you should learn to write one-page summaries of your work for those instances when the boss needs information fast. You can use this approach even when you're not in a hurry.

The object is to communicate efficiently and save the boss's time. This can be done with a note. It does not have to be typewritten or perfect in format. You can simply write it longhand on a memo pad and send it to the boss. I can assure you that busy people will appreciate your consideration and, if you are a boss, you will like to have something in writing as well.

# Rule 5: Don't Break the Chain of Command

There is a chain of command in every organization. This is the line of authority from the top to the bottom defining who works for whom. It is also the prescribed route for sending communications from bottom to top.

"Chain of command" is a military term and civilians don't like to use it, particularly in the private sector. Some workers prefer "management structure" or even "hierarchy." No matter; the chain of command exists in civilian as well as military organizations.

It would be unwise to believe that there is any less insistence on adherence to the chain of command in civilian organizations than there is in the military. I have served in both, and my opinion is that civilian organizations are even more insistent on the proper protocols than military organizations. This goes for private companies as well as for the government.

Using the chain of command means that all work, documents, suggestions, questions, and requests travel from the lowest level through the prescribed organizational structure. Everything passes from the worker to the branch chief, division chief, deputy director, director, principal director, deputy assistant secretary, principal deputy assistant secretary, assistant secretary, under secretary, deputy secretary, and finally, the secretary. This is a typical federal agency chain of command. A private-sector chain of command might go from the worker to the team leader, project manager, deputy program director, program director, assistant vice president, vice president, senior vice president, executive vice president, and finally, the company president. There are variations depending on the organizational idiosyncracies and titles assumed by the organization. Notice that I have inserted all of the "assistants" and "deputies" in the chain. In organizational theory taught by the best business schools, assistants and deputies are supposed to be substitutes and helpers on the same level as their principals. In practice the assistants and deputies are a separate approval/disapproval level, and they want to be consulted on the way up and informed on the way down.

Going through the chain of command is tedious, time consuming, and frustrating. This tempts some enterprising workers or midlevel managers to break the chain of command. They try to skip one of the approval/disapproval levels in the official organizational structure. A worker might ignore his or her branch chief and take a request directly to the division chief. Or the branch chief might go directly to the director, skipping the division chief and deputy director. This is called "making an end run." Actually, when a worker or lowly branch chief hops all the way to an assistant secretary or vice president without going through each wicket along the way, it is more like the office equivalent of "throwing a bomb."

Breaking the chain of command may get some instant relief but is dangerous and will be counterproductive later. You might be able to get faster action one or two times, but you will suffer thereafter. Even the higher official who listens to you as you are breaking the chain does not really approve of what you are doing. He or she likes the comfort of knowing that your idea or your numbers have been vetted (a great word—look it up) by intermediate managers. Those intermediate managers will be angry. Not only have you robbed them of their right to review, revise, reprove, and cavil, but you have insulted their position. You have shown them no respect, and that is a cardinal sin in a hierarchy.

So my advice is to forget all that about breaking the chain of command. Even if the executive vice president is your brother-in-law, don't do it. It will gain you little in the long run and you may even become known as a troublemaker. So stick to it. Go through the wickets and bide your time. You may get to be a wicket yourself one day.

Oh, yes. If you just happen to have a frank talk with your brother-in-law, the executive vice president, during Thanksgiving dinner, who's to know?

# Pay and Leave

Next to the boss, the most important thing about your work is compensation—your pay and benefits. Just because you are a link in the chain doesn't mean that you will work for nothing, or even for peanuts. In fact, pay, retirement, leave, and the other elements of your employee benefits package are very important to you and to your job satisfaction.

One of the bad things about being an office worker is that it is hard to look back after a hard day's work and have something concrete to show for it. Workers who produce something tangible don't have this problem. Construction workers see their product rise before them. Production workers feel and fondle the cars, rugs, cloth, or other goods they make. Even service workers get satisfaction from serving a meal or handing back clean laundry. But office workers seldom produce anything tangible. They make (or help to make) policy, they run projects, and they manage programs. Their victories are small—a paragraph in a company manual, a sentence in a speech made by the secretary of something, a document approved for publication. So it is hard for most organization workers to see what they produce, and this leads to great interest in compensation as the tangible rewards of the job.

There is a great difference between public- and private-sector compensation. In the public sector pay scales are published and the benefits are known to all. In government everyone knows exactly what everyone else is making. In the private sector compensation is closely held. Employees deal individually with their bosses and the personnel office on pay and benefits, and this is all highly confidential. In the private sector no one knows what other people are earning, or at least this is the policy. In practice, of course, there are great efforts made to learn what co-workers and others are making, since this establishes a pecking order. For all workers, public and private, compensation is a very important part of the job, so the next set of rules deals with how to approach these compensation matters.

## Rule 6: Read Your Pay Slip

You probably take your pay for granted. This is a mistake. You should know all about your pay—gross per pay period, hourly rate, how much is being taken out for the Federal Insurance Contributions Act (Medicare only or both Medicare and Old-Age and Survivor Benefits), retirement, federal and state income tax withholding, savings bonds, medical insurance, group life insurance, or any other deduction. It is your money and you should know what is happening to it.

It is unlikely that the pay system will make an error, but this does happen sometimes due to a change in status such as a promotion or a transfer. Generally speaking, if the personnel system sends the right information to payroll, the pay will be correct.

However, personnel is not always perfect, and one way to check to see if your personnel action went through is to see if its effects show up on the pay slip. Then again, it is just prudent to take a few seconds to see that your pay is correct.

There is more to it than just detecting errors. If you are a good financial manager, you will be calculating your federal and state taxes so that you will get the amount of refund that you want. Some people want to get a big refund and arrange their withholding so that they pay too much tax along the way. Others try to have their withholding equal their tax so they neither get a refund nor pay more taxes. No one deliberately plans to have a large tax payment along with the Form 1040 because this causes a cash crunch in April, and there are penalties and interest if you do not withhold enough taxes during the year. Most workers, unfortunately, don't even know what this paragraph is about. Too many employees pay attention only to their take-home pay and fail to understand gross pay and deductions.

So another reason to check each pay slip is to get a feel for how your total income is being spent. You are paying into a retirement system of one kind or another. You are paying income taxes as you earn. You are contributing to some savings. You are purchasing life and health insurance. These expenditures should be figured into your overall spending. That is why a careful worker knows where every penny goes.

# Rule 7: Know When You Can Retire

One of the important items that every experienced worker should know is when he or she can retire. I don't mean generally, like in the 21st century or in twenty years. I mean to the minute. There is a great difference between government and private-sector retirement benefits, so retirement will be discussed under two headings.

## Federal Government Retirement

One of the best things about federal employment is its generous retirement system. The "old" Civil Service Retirement System is one of the best staff retirement systems around. It is designed to encourage people to enter the civil service at an early age and stay for a full thirty-year career. For these career employees, CSRS is very good indeed. In fact, the very goodness of CSRS has led to its downfall. Congress, aided by interest groups who thought that civil servants had it too good, has put into effect a new retirement system, the Federal Employees Retirement System.

FERS was intended to save money. Unless there actually is a free lunch, it cannot be as good as CSRS, at least for long-time employees, and it isn't. FERS is designed to shift some of the burden of financing retirement to the employee. This was done by cutting the pension part of the package about in half, placing federal employees under Social Security, and allowing the employees to contribute to a tax-deferred retirement plan. If an employee contributes to his or her retirement, the government also will contribute. Overall, the benefits for identical service are about the same in the two systems, but they are financed in different ways.

FERS is better for people who enter and leave government rather than stay an entire career. This is called portability, and it means that people who leave government service without a full career can carry with them some retirement benefits, primarily Social Security and the tax-deferred savings plan. The effect will be to promote turnover in the federal work force, which was intended. Turnover means "fresh blood" to some personnel managers.

All federal employees hired or rehired after January 1987 are covered by FERS automatically. Congress also allowed old employees to transfer from CSRS to FERS during an open season from July 1, 1987, to December 31, 1987, and even later. The response was underwhelming. Almost all employees who were covered by the older system elected to remain in it, so the systems will coexist until all of the old-timers retire.

I instructed federal employees on the virtues and vices of the two systems. The general ignorance of most employees about their own futures was startling. These people were being asked to make what was likely the most important financial decision they would ever make, and many did not have the faintest idea about their entitlements.

Of course, some workers did know about their retirement and had calculated the advantages and disadvantages of the plans. These people understood that in order to assure their benefits, they had to learn about them.

It is no good just waiting for the personnel people to take care of you. You have to know not only when you can retire but what you are going to receive. The rules are so complicated, particularly with FERS, and turnover so great among retirement counselors that the system is not likely to be able to give you the right information.

Retirement is one of the things workers are entitled to when they work for the federal government. The old compact was that you traded off possibly higher pay for job security and a comfortable retirement. That compact has been disturbed by FERS, but it still exists.

To make wise career choices, you have to know your options. That means you should know to the minute when you can retire, and what that means for you financially. This is hard for young people, who do not plan to grow old, but it is smart to learn these things now to avoid disappointment later on.

This discussion has dwelled on federal retirement systems, but there are also good retirement systems for employees of states and local governments. There also is a wide variety, so each state and local worker should understand the contributions, benefits, and ins and outs of his or her system.

## Private-Sector Retirement

There is great variety among private-sector retirement benefits. Some large companies have elaborate retirement systems like the federal one. Some companies rely on tax-deferred savings plans to which they contribute. Other companies make no provision at all for employee retirement. So it is even more important for you private-sector workers to know what retirement benefits are offered by your company.

Although younger people don't like to think about it much, humans age, and they get tired and less eager to be at the office at 8:15 A.M. every weekday. So there must come a time for them to retire. To many people the prospect of retirement is pleasing and they look forward to days of golf, travel, hobbies, civic activities, or just fun. To other people the office is the most important aspect of their life, and they dread retirement, not knowing what they will do with all the free time. Regardless, both groups have one thing is common—they will need money to live on in retirement.

Your private-sector retirement will have three foundations: Social Security, your company's plan, and your savings.

Most of you will have Social Security. You are paying the FICA tax, and provided you have forty quarters of covered employment, you will be able to get a monthly check starting at age sixty-two. This check will not be much compared with your active earnings, however, so you shouldn't rely on it for your entire retirement. Social Security is a complicated system, and you have to take the time to learn about it. You can obtain general information, receive a record of your own contributions over your working life and an estimate of your benefits from the Social Security Administration. Simply call the local Social Security office and get instructions.

If your company has a retirement system, use it. Take the reduced take-home pay even though it may seem to be a hardship now. Doing without luxuries while you are working is better than doing without necessities when you are retired. Join the 401(k) plan (tax-deferred savings) or the company retirement plan. Buy stock and stock options if they are offered at a discount. Let management know that you are interested in your future. Many companies have benefit plans that allow workers to emphasize the benefits they value particularly—leave, health insurance, and retirement—and don't overlook retirement.

The final way to provide for your golden years is to have your own savings and investment program. This calls for some bravery. You don't have any choice about Social Security, and contributing to the company retirement plan may seem natural. But few workers, particularly the younger ones, have the discipline to save from their take-home pay. This is not a book on finance or mental courage, so it will suffice to say that saving now for retirement is a wise, although not necessarily exciting, course.

My advice for all office workers is to think now about how well you are going to live when you retire.

# Rule 8: Take Your Annual Leave

One of your most important benefits is annual leave or vacation. It is particularly important for office workers who need to get away to recharge their batteries and make a sanity check.

Compared with leave benefits in most private companies, the federal plan is generous. Most federal employees earn eighty hours of leave per year. New people earn less and some old-timers earn more. Since leave time counts only against workdays, you have almost a month of leave coming to you (including holidays), depending on how you take it. General schedule, general managerial, and wage grade employees may accrue up to 240 hours of leave, but once that number is exceeded, they lose the excess at the end of the calendar year.

Annual leave for employees of private companies varies a great deal. Most companies require a new employee to work for a year or even more before becoming eligible for leave. Two weeks per year is usual, but some companies give longer leave allowances for decades of dedicated service. Of course, all workers enjoy getting paid holidays.

It is important to know how much leave you earn and how much you have accrued. This information is on your payroll slip or leave and earnings statement, which is made available after each pay period. Study it and know your leave situation.

Once you find out how much annual leave you have coming, you have to decide what to do about it. My advice is to take your annual leave every year. That is, take the full eighty hours or whatever in the year in which it is earned. There are few good reasons to save up annual leave and none to lose any. You may wish to accrue the maximum annual leave and then take it as you earn it. This will allow you to get a cash payment for the accrued leave when you retire or change jobs, so there is at least a reason to get to the maximum and stay there.

You should never, never, never lose any leave. That is just wasting money. Some workers believe that there is virtue in losing leave. This is like flogging yourself. It is a good sign of fanaticism, but it calls into question your mental state. Waiting too long to schedule leave and then finding yourself boxed in so that you lose it is a classic self-inflicted wound.

There are many reasons to take leave. One reason is that life is short and you should smell the roses along the way. Also, spouses and children deserve time and attention. You also may need time for household chores, although some people consider this a reason *not* to take leave. The most important reason is to maintain your mental and physical health.

Working in a large organization is stressful. Regardless of appearances, there is a lot of tension in an office job. Most people try to do a good job and they often must work under adverse circumstances. Congress micromanages. The board of directors wants instant profits. There are more auditors and investigators than workers. Government regulations are frustrating and the forms are impossible to do correctly. The Office of Management and Budget stalls on everything. Your big bosses waffle and change their minds. Your own boss rewrites everything. Your co-workers have their own agendas and the other offices fight over turf, position, and policy. It's a jungle in there.

So you need to get away, relax, and contemplate your navel. You need to refresh and do other things for a while. That is why you get annual leave and why most bosses encourage you to take it. It allows you to remain sane and hearty and ultimately to return to the job ready to go full-steam again.

## Rule 9: Schedule Your Leave Well in Advance

Every office does it! Sometime in the fall, a slip will be circulated asking each employee to fill out his or her desired leave dates. This is to allow the boss or, more likely, the Dragon (see Rule 80) to schedule everyone's vacation.

The leave schedule is important to the boss. He or she does not want all of the key players to be out of the office at the same time. The boss does not want working strength reduced at known crunch times. He or she wants to manage the darned thing.

This depends on your cooperation. If you simply fail to fill out the leave schedule or put down an arbitrary date, you have caused a problem—especially when you finally make up your mind and ask for leave. Since your request is not on the schedule, it is an "unprogrammed demand." A bureaucracy does not like unprogrammed demands and does not deal well with them. So your sudden or short-notice request is unlikely to bring cheer to the front office. You will have to be fitted into the leave schedule, and you are unlikely to get what you want. This will make you angry, so failing to put in your leave request or, worse, faking it at the start is simply not good form.

Your whole year can be improved by planning your annual leave well in advance and giving honest, firm dates when asked. Planning well in advance will also allow your spouse, kids, and others to set their schedules. It means that you can tie into other known events, such as school vacations and condo availability. It allows you to take control of your leave.

Planning and scheduling in advance also helps you to get your leave when you want it. Those who have trips set, reservations made, and deposits sent are less likely to have their plans upset by sudden workload perils. It is hard for the boss to upset well-laid plans, though this happens more often than some people like.

So you should treat your annual leave as a valuable asset and use it well. This means playing ball when the leave schedule request is circulated.

## Rule 10: Take Sick Leave Only If You Are Ill

Most organizations have a generous sick leave policy. Federal employees accrue seventy-two sick leave hours per year and continue to accrue sick leave until they retire. Most companies provide one or two weeks of sick leave per year. This allows an employee to receive pay while attending medical appointments or suffering from short illnesses.

Unfortunately, sick leave is sometimes abused by the less

productive members of an organization. Some people "ride" the sick book by taking sick leave when they are not really sick.

Supervisors know these people, such as the employee with a sailboat who gets sick frequently on Fridays and Mondays during good sailing weather. In general, there is a surge in sick leave on Fridays and Mondays in order to gain precious three-day weekends. Employees who claim they are sick when it is obvious they are not show that they are dishonest and unreliable.

Federal employees covered by CSRS have an incentive to save sick leave. Accrued sick leave can be applied to years of service for computing pension benefits. This rewards healthy and honest workers with more money when they retire. The rules have been changed under FERS. Sick leave may be accrued but not applied to increase a pension. The betting is that FERS employees will take a lot more sick leave than CSRS employees.

Of course, honest people will take sick leave only when they need it, so you should be scrupulous about sick leave. Don't lie about being ill so you can get an unearned day off. Use your annual leave for days off and use your sick leave for being sick.

## Rule 11: Take Sick Leave When You Are Ill

The other side of this sick leave business is that you should take it when you are ill. Some conscientious workers won't stay in bed even when they need to. This happens a lot during hot projects and before big deadlines, such as putting a budget to bed. People come to work with fevers, chills, and stuffed-up noses, just to name some milder symptoms. They believe that there is virtue in working sick.

There may be some excuse for coming to work when you really should stay home, but only rarely. Most of the time, all you do is spread your disease around to the healthy workers. A lot of influenza is spread this way, and probably other diseases, too. So one reason to stay home when you are sick is out of consideration for the health of your co-workers.

Another reason is that you may not do your best work when

you are ill. Headaches, sore throats, and watery eyes are not the prescription for the best speech, the best analysis, or the best typing. Showing up but doing poor work because of your ill health is not a good deal for the boss.

The most important reason to take sick leave when you need it is to conserve your health and your energies for the long haul. You are going to be around for many years, most likely, and your most important asset is your good health. You jeopardize it when you disregard doctor's instructions and try to do too much. Relax, follow orders, stay in bed (or whatever), and get well so that you can return to work full of vigor.

# Your Office Is Your Castle

You probably spend more time at work than at home, except for weekends and federal holidays. So the physical environment of your workplace has to be important to you. You don't have much choice about your building or even your office, but there are a lot of things that you can do to make your working environment pleasant, which will improve your productivity.

This set of rules is on making your office your castle. Particular attention has been paid to that office necessity, your desk.

## Rule 12: Be at Home in Your Office

You should make yourself at home at the office. This means that you should try to create an atmosphere that is warm, inviting, and friendly—a place in which you are comfortable and can do good work.

To achieve this kind of "homey" atmosphere, you should decorate your office. Bring in some photographs of your spouse and kids. Hang a picture or plaque—maybe a poster, if it is not too garish. Have a nameplate and various other kinds of curios and personal items. A radio or clock might be nice. Perhaps you might like fake or real flowers. Perhaps green plants would look nice. The idea is to fix up the place.

Of course, you can go overboard on this fairly quickly. You could make the place so inviting and warm that you do nothing but sleep. So you have to exercise good judgment and taste on what you do and how much you decorate. Don't line the walls with revealing shots from *Playboy* or *Playgirl*. Don't put in too much kitsch. Avoid a twenty-five-inch TV set unless you need it in your work. Don't put in a garden. In short, don't go to excess. If you exceed the bounds of good taste or propriety, your boss will undoubtedly let you know.

This is an area, by the way, on which most bosses have fixed opinions. Most are relatively lenient and allow employees to fix up their spaces pretty much as they please, as long as they are relatively neat and there is some space left for working.

Some bosses, however, are adamant about forbidding any decoration. These bosses issue edicts about hanging pictures or having any personal items. They want a functional look—bare walls and no frills. These bosses believe that an austere environment is good for workers, when in fact the opposite is true. If you are unlucky enough to have a bare-wall boss, lie back and wait. He will be moving along soon.

On the other hand, bosses have to take a strong position sometimes when workers overdo it. I remember when we moved from an old building to a new one, the workers tried to re-create the familiar and rather dowdy atmosphere of their old quarters. In the old building there were no partitions, so over a period of about fifteen years, the workers had ingeniously fashioned cubicles out of bookshelves. There was no rhyme or reason to the layout, and the sight of all of those bookshelves filled with dusty old regulations and forgotten reports was really awesome. It resembled a Hollywood version of a Dickensian library.

The new building was clean, bright, well laid out, and offered an opportunity to advance 200 years in office decor. However, initially left to their own devices, the employees simply re-created in the building the atmosphere of the old building with their partitions of bookshelves and the same dusty tomes. On my initial visit to the offices after the move, I was horrified and ordered peremptorily that the bookshelf walls come down. Soon the offices were relatively clean, spacious, and logically arranged. There was much grumbling, but the results were worth it.

As with anything like this, there are employees who tend to spoil it for the rest. The employees who create junkyards out of their offices or who turn them into boutiques invite the bosses to crack down on decorations. My advice is to make yourself at home, but not too much so.

## Rule 13: Have a Hold Drawer

Every successful worker needs a spacious hold drawer. The only way for an office worker to survive the blizzard of paper is to have a method for sorting it out. This requires a kind of paper-work triage—separating all letters, memos, manuals, papers, regulations, and reports into three basic categories:

1. **Quick stuff.** These are the papers that you can deal with immediately. You read or sign them or do whatever is required and put them immediately into your out box. (The virtues of an out box will be covered in the next rule.)

2. **Too-hard stuff.** These are the papers that you find immediately distasteful. They are too long, too complicated, too filled with equations or italicized prose, or simply too far out. Since you have no intention of dealing with them, the proper response for too-hard stuff is also to put them into your out box. You will have to face the moral issue of whether to initial them or not. Since an initial implies that you have read or at least glanced at the document, placing your initials on it states that you know what is inside. On the other hand, if you don't initial the distribution slip, the darned thing might come back to you courtesy of an overzealous mail clerk. I am not going to solve this ethical question; I'll just say that the proper thing to do with too-hard stuff is to put it into the out box.

3. **Not-now stuff.** These are the papers that you really want

to read but cannot find the time, energy, or inspiration to tackle right now. The proper place to put these documents is in your hold box or hold drawer.

I find that the best place for a hold box is the middle drawer on the left-hand side of the desk. Since I am left-handed, it is very convenient to glance at a paper and then with one graceful motion open the drawer and deposit the paper on top of the stack. Done properly, few observers will appreciate the true significance of this holding tactic. For right-handed people the best drawer might be the middle right-hand drawer, except that many office desks have a file drawer on the bottom right. File drawers are not good for hold boxes because they are too big.

Having a hold box right up on top of the desk is not recommended for most people. Only masochists and eager beavers do this. A hold box on the desk displays to all the work that you should have done but have deferred. No matter how noble your motives or how justified your delay, this will work against you. Everyone will note that you have a substantial stack of unread reports and memos. This will irritate both your supervisor and your co-workers, but for different reasons.

Moreover, having a hold box piled high on the desk makes it hard to get away with the clean "in" box trick.

If you work with sensitive or classified information in a secure area, you will have to put your hold box in the safe each night. This is perfect cover for procrastination.

Once you have started using a desk-drawer hold box, the first few weeks or months are wonderful. You can have a clean desk and a clear conscience, for you really mean to read the stuff. Once the desk drawer fills up, however, you will have to face the moment of truth. You have not done what you promised yourself you would do. You have not read the stuff.

When this happens, the only thing to do is to dump the contents of the hold drawer on the desk. Do this when your supervisor is on leave or at least at lunch. By dumping the stack upside down, you will be able to operate under the first-in, first-out principle, which is highly recommended.

One of the wonderful things about this approach is that you

will find that a sizable proportion of the papers are OBE—"overtaken by events." You will not have to decide to attend the luncheon for old Charley's retirement because it was two weeks ago. You will not have to decline to donate blood because the blood drive is over. You will not have to provide that important report to your boss because you missed the deadline. Oops!

That illustrates the importance of paperwork triage. Holding things is generally good, because it helps separate the wheat from the chaff, but it also leads to an occasional big blunder. Unless you want to read all of that stuff on the bus or in the car pool, you will just have to take a chance.

A hold drawer is part of your mental survival gear. You should make good use of it, but don't overdo it.

# Rule 14: Don't Have a Clean Desktop—Except at Night

Desks are a source of opportunity and risk. The appearance of a desk tells a lot about the person using it.

A desk is a real asset to an office worker. It is almost an essential tool. It provides a barrier against intrusion. It provides a flat area to work on or spread papers on. It provides nooks and crannies in which to cache supplies, papers, and personal items. It allows you to get organized or to hide the disorganization. It is hard to imagine how you could get along without one.

One of the best things about a desk is that it can conceal so many things. It can hide that handy hold drawer. It can hold tissues, spare birthday cards, extra shoes, socks, and other items not to be kept out in the open. It can hold pencils, pens, erasers, paper clips, binder clips, memo pads, and all of the other tools of office work. It can hold lunches (hopefully on a short-term basis), snacks, and cigarettes to sustain and nourish the occupant. It can even hold some files and precious documents. A desk can hold these things with an air of absolute neatness—once the drawers are closed.

I have to caution at this point that it is highly discourteous to get into another worker's drawers without permission. Not only is this a serious breach of privacy, but it is apt to be highly disillusioning. From time to time I have had to look into drawers of strange desks—furtively and hastily, of course. Most of the time, the drawers reveal chaos and confusion, and even the most organized people have one "crazy" drawer into which they dump things that do not fit neatly into another bin. So avoid drawers not your own unless absolutely necessary.

The part of the desk that cannot be concealed is is the top. This is the crucial area. Your work habits and your seriousness will be judged to a great extent by the contents and arrangement of your desktop, so there are several rules that apply here.

This rule is to avoid a clean desk during working hours. This may seem to be a contrary view at first. A clean desk could be assumed to be the mark of a highly organized and efficient worker. After all, what could be more organized than nothing? A clean desk, with nothing showing except the costly desk set with token pens and an unstained blotter, and perhaps a discreet nameplate, certainly looks nice. However, an empty desk gives the impression that you simply are not doing any work.

Clean desktops have become the hallmark of certain high-level bureaucrats. The supplicant enters the room, which looks as if it has been decorated by a Spartan, and approaches the clean desk humbly, where the great man or woman sits and knows all without ever referring to a note or memo. This is impressive, but most people cannot get away with it. I wager that all of these clean desk exhibitionists have a secret room next door in which the papers and memos are strewn around just like the rest of us do, or at least that the desk drawers are a real mess. At any rate, the clean desk is a luxury that only really top officials can afford. (This affectation is related to the table desk and the stand-up desk, which are discussed elsewhere.)

For most of us, therefore, it is necessary to use our desks for real work. This implies spreading papers out and arranging stacks, and even having one or more in, out, or hold boxes on the desktop. It implies a degree of disorder, which is really order, according to our own work habits. So I urge you not to be too orderly at your desk during the daytime. Really use the thing for its intended purpose. You will get the benefit of the doubt about working, and you might actually get something done.

It is usually good, however, to straighten up the desktop somewhat just before quitting time. Leaving the desk in its customary disorder is easy, but after hours it looks just plain sloppy rather than clever. So take the last few minutes of the workday and bring some order to the desktop. This is a good time to feed your hold drawer and to get a start on the next day's work by arranging papers into piles.

If you work in a sensitive or classified environment, you will have to clear the desktop completely each night. This is good and bad. It's good because it minimizes the risk of leaving a classified document out, but it's bad because the normal way to do this is to pile all desktop documents into a hold box and stick them into the safe. This makes the first minutes of the next workday quite interesting as you try to sort out what happened. So even in a classified environment, sort out the papers on the desktop before securing them.

The main point is that your desk is a workplace and you should work on it. Remember that your desktop is a pretty good reflection of your personality and your approach to work.

## Rule 15: Don't Have a Messy Desktop—Anytime

The other side of the coin is that you should always avoid having a really messy desktop. The art of the desktop is to show enough activity to convince your boss and co-workers that you are really working, but to do so in a semiorganized manner. Thus, it is necessary to walk a fine line between unconvincing neatness and sloppy disorder. This is not easy.

Some people excuse a sloppy desktop by saying that *they* know where everything is and can put their hands on it instantaneously. That is, there is order in chaos. While this is in consonance with one of the latest mathematical discoveries and may even be true, it is not convincing. There is no consensus on what is an unacceptably sloppy desk, but most people know one when they see one. Immense stacks of documents, books, files, folders, magazines, and even newspapers on a desktop, arranged in random order or worse, indicate a sloppy desk. The stacks are leaning, and some of the stuff has even fallen to the floor. There is a small work space cleared out, but the blotter thus revealed is covered with graffiti or even blots. The telephone is nearly obscured, to be extricated only with difficulty when used, and then discarded casually back into the piles. You have seen such desks. Mostly they belong to accredited eccentrics whose work is so valuable or so dimly understood that they and their sloppy desktops are accepted grudgingly. Noneccentrics, however, can't get away with this.

So unless you have achieved eccentric status, my advice is to maintain some degree of order on your desktop. If it gets disorderly during the day, hew to Rule 14 about clearing it off before leaving. With some effort you can even maintain order during the working day. This involves appropriate use of the hold box or drawer, taking some time to organize your thoughts and papers, and making and sticking to a "do list." Your desktop may or may not reflect accurately your state of mind, but lacking other evidence, your boss and co-workers may think you're orderly. At least give that appearance.

## Rule 16: Get Away from Your Desk

A desk is a wonderful thing. It is a place of comfort and warmth that takes on the very personality of the user after a while. So it is understandable that office workers are reluctant to leave that security for the dangers of the world.

In fact, a clever person need never leave his or her desk except for necessities such as coffee, lunch, the bathroom, and an occasional staff meeting. Most work can be done at the desk, and communication can be maintained by telephone. Thus, many people tend to stay at their desks even when there is nothing to do.

Unfortunately, a desk can also be an excuse for inaction and isolation. The rest of the world of work is not nearly as safe or familiar as your desk, so the temptation is strong to stay put rather than move around.

My advice is to get away from your desk. Make a conscious effort to move out from behind the protective barrier, out of your office and into the dangerous world beyond. Do this even if there is work or make-work that could serve as an excuse to remain at the desk and dawdle. Do this deliberately as part of your effort to remain in touch with reality.

If you are a boss, you should sally forth to visit your people to see for yourself what they are doing. There is nothing better than having the boss drop in unannounced or announced. The good workers will welcome your attention; the poor workers will work harder. You will notice things that you cannot see huddled in your office behind that desk. You might find out what is really going on. Don't limit this to your initial orientation visit; that is merely ritual. Visit periodically during your tenure as boss.

You should also visit your peers. Recognizing the limitations of telephonic communication, you should make a habit of visiting your opposite numbers in other parts of the organization. This is called networking nowadays, and it is a good idea. Get away from your desk and go to see your peers in their own offices. In this case it is judicious to make an appointment. This minimizes your risk of a dry run and allows the visitee to get ready mentally, or at least straighten up his or her desktop.

You should also make an effort to visit your boss and your boss's boss. This obviously has some wrinkles that do not apply to visiting your own people or peers. Despite some risks of seeming to be pushy or even toadying, go to see the bosses. This should be done when you have something of value to say or when you need guidance. Simply go to the front office if your status permits you to pass the Dragon and see the boss for the short time it takes to deliver the message or get the word. If you are not in favor with the Dragon, make an appointment. Bosses will appreciate hearing from you and seeing you, and (depending on your message) will welcome your visit. For one thing, it allows them to get some human contact without having to leave their own offices.

The major point is that the desk can be a fortress protecting you from the reality of the world; it can be a sanctuary. But if you succumb to the temptation of security and familiarity by never leaving your desk, you are shortchanging yourself. Using the desk as a base of operations, sally forth to present yourself in person to your people, your peers, and your bosses. Make the effort.

# Rule 17: Stay Loose on Moving

It is necessary to talk a bit about moving. It seems that office workers are always moving. This is true for private-sector employees as well as government employees. This naturally affects your office and your serenity, to say nothing about your productivity.

For some strange reason, just as soon as you get settled comfortably into your office and are ready to roll, the moving team shows up. Usually, you have no warning and are simply tossed some empty boxes and given cryptic instructions about Room X or Area D. You pack hastily, the movers clean everything out, and you are without an office. The next step is to find your new office, which is always worse than your old office. If you are really lucky, the new office, which needs painting and a clean carpet, will have your stuff in it when you arrive. If you are just normally lucky, your stuff will show up in a few days. If you are unlucky, you will never see your old stuff.

Moving is a way of life and most people accept it as a condition of employment, like time cards and bosses. Some people resist it and get really fed up. I remember one rather senior employee who got very upset after his third unscheduled move in three months. After the third move he simply refused to unpack or to take the name tags off the boxes. His office was really a sight, with tags on his desk, computer, and chair, and all his books and papers neatly packed in boxes in the corner. He was hard to do business with, for the first twenty minutes of every conversation was about office moving. At least he was ready to move again. Knowing the system, however, I suspect he is sitting there still in his office waiting for the moving team, but to no avail. Only those people who don't want to move are actually moved.

This brings up the question of why people move. Some suspect that there is a covert move-planning section in corporate headquarters or the White House that sees that no worker stays longer than twelve months in the same office. This may not be true, but the effect is the same. Moving is done, according to the bosses, to provide unit integrity for the branches, divisions, and directorates. It's supposed to be good to have all of the people working for one boss clustered in the same area. This would probably be true except that there is nothing more volatile than an organization chart. It is so easy to move people around on a piece of paper that the bosses do this constantly under the illusion that they are improving things. This is particularly true for the new boss, who apparently needs to reorganize shortly after his or her ascension, merely to show who's boss. Well, it may be easy to shuffle names on paper, but the effect is that the offices, desks, computers, and all the rest of an office worker's paraphernalia will also have to be shuffled, and that is work!

The only good thing about office moving is that it shows conclusively that management can keep a secret if it really wants to. Extracts from TOP SECRET military plans appear in the newspapers regularly, as do closely held personnel appointments. Balance sheets and sales projections are highlighted in the *Wall Street Journal*. Studies critical of the government are discussed by TV pundits regularly, but no one knows in advance when the office move will occur. The security for moves is really good. The first hint that the hapless employee gets is when the moving team shows up at his or her door. Often this surprises even the boss, who has to ask around to find where his people are located.

My advice on moving is to relax and enjoy it. There is nothing you can do about it. While I don't recommend leaving all of your possessions in packing boxes, you can at least stay loose enough to move on a moment's notice. This will help to keep the sheer amount of your things limited and it will force you to decide what is really important. You can rationalize this whole subject by just considering moves to be realistic rehearsals of the continuity of operations plan.

# Telephones

Next to a desk your most important tool is the telephone. Don Ameche had no idea of the terrible forces he was unleashing on the world when he invented the telephone. This instrument has caused more trouble, achieved more results, and taken more time than any other technological innovation in the history of government and commerce. Even the typewriter and the copier—both office gangbusters—have not had the impact of the telephone. So it is not only appropriate but mandatory to have a set of rules on how to use it.

It is the telephone that is really to blame for the rise of BIG—big business and big government. It allows XYZ Corporation and the federal government to extend their tentacles into each household in America. The telephone facilitates coordination so that deals, policies, campaigns, regulations, and actions that formerly took months can now be accomplished in days or even hours. The telephone lets everyone get involved in the simplest matter. It permits decentralized implementation as well as centralized command and control.

So it is natural that office workers have to master this tool

quickly, for the newest challenge to their ingenuity is the facsimile machine, or fax, which is likely to revolutionize office work
just as thoroughly as the telephone did. Here are a few basic rules
for telephony and just a hint about faxing.

## Rule 18: Use the Telephone Properly

The telephone is the omnipresent tool of government and commerce. You probably spend much of your day on the phone, so
learning how to use it properly is a necessary office skill.

It is amazing that almost all people talk on the telephone
without any training. The phone is a sophisticated communication device, but most people think they can operate it without
any instruction. They hesitate to operate a microwave oven without studying the manual; they do not even turn on a popcorn
popper without reading the instructions carefully, but they pick
up the phone and just charge in. Even driving, another innate
American ability, requires some basic study and, increasingly,
some formal instruction. Ability to use a telephone, many people
apparently believe, is obtained from an obscure but dominant
gene.

Using a telephone is really not that easy, however, and care-
less talking on the phone can be dangerous. You may irritate the
person on the other end without knowing it. It is easy to get off
on the wrong foot on the telephone, especially when talking to
strangers. So it is important to be civil and restrained when doing
business by telephone, particularly on the initial call.

My advice is to never use the phone for business that is really
important. For the truly hot stuff, do it in person. It is too easy to
misunderstand each other over a telephone, and it is too easy to
create friction and antagonism over a telephone line without
meaning to.

Talking over a telephone is one-dimensional. The only thing
that can be heard are the words, the tone, and the nuances of
speech. These suffice for routine communication, but the additional elements of body language and facial expression are
needed to convey the full message. Of course, it is impossible to
transmit large amounts of data efficiently over the telephone

orally. There is too much chance of error in conveying numbers over the phone, for instance, and some things have to be written. So you can do a more complete, more efficient, and more accurate job of communicating in person.

More important even than that, however, is that there is much room for creating animosity over the phone that doesn't appear in most personal encounters. Strangers often take callers to be rude or arrogant, even though they don't mean to be. If at all possible, you should go to see people on important matters. Once you create a personal bond with a face-to-face meeting, it usually is safe to do business on the telephone. If you cannot do that, then you should take extra care to use the telephone properly. The rules are simple:

1. Identify yourself and your office right away.

2. State the purpose of your call so that the other person can start thinking of a response.

3. Get to the point politely and don't waste time. This is best done with people you know well.

4. Spend some time on small talk at first when talking to strangers. This creates a climate of cordiality and trust when you start talking business.

5. Maintain a neutral tone and a soft voice. It is not necessary to yell when talking long distance, though many people still do.

6. Never get angry over the phone and never hang up. You are separated by distance and you will have a hard time mending the breach of trust caused by harsh words over the phone. It is particularly insulting for you to hang up on the other party.

You should practice good telephone manners so that you can communicate better. Just don't take the telephone for granted.

You should never play "telephone tag." This is a game played by some senior people lucky enough to have a secretary to place and receive calls. The object of the game is to force the other person to get on the line before you do. This is supposed to give the winner more points in the prestige contest.

Here's how it goes. Mr. X says to his secretary: "Get Ms. Y on the line." The secretary calls Ms. Y's secretary and says, "Mr. X is calling." Or, if this is really sophisticated, "Is Ms. Y in for Mr. X?"

Ms. Y's secretary buzzes her and says, "Mr. X is calling." Normal protocol is for the caller, Mr. X, to get on the line when the connection is going through, so that Ms. Y will be talking directly to Mr. X when she picks up the phone. Telephone tag comes in when Ms. Y picks up the phone and hears Mr. X's secretary say, "I'll put Mr. X on the line." Ms. Y has been outmaneuvered and has lost face by getting on the line first. Twenty-five points to Mr. X.

Some senior people become obsessed with this, as if to make public exhibition of their position. There is no rational basis for it. The time spent waiting for secretaries to maneuver is lost to both executives. Several studies and books by top managers imply that it is faster to place the calls yourself rather than have the secretary do it. I don't know about that, but I do know that playing ego games about who gets on the line first is not useful. The really important people whom I admire for their general good work do not engage in this foolishness.

## Rule 19: Return Phone Calls

One measure of clout in a large organization is getting a phone call returned. You know you are really someone if the vice president or assistant secretary returns your calls. That means you are deemed important enough by the great person or his or her Dragon to be worthy of a return call.

One thing you can do to advance the cause of civilization is to return all of your telephone calls promptly and courteously. This will not be easy. It takes time and effort, even if you are so fortunate as to have a secretary to place the calls. Moreover, some of the calls will simply be a waste of time. You will receive calls from peers seeking information, from bosses seeking information, and from subordinates seeking information. You will also be pestered by contractors, consultants, and clients seeking work. Finally, you will be receiving calls from citizens either complaining or asking for help or both. No matter how silly the call is or how much you dread talking to a particular person, you should do it. It is part of the job.

For one thing, you avoid sending a rejection notice to your caller. You are telling the caller that he or she is important enough for you to make the effort to return the call. This is good. It is good for the caller, and it may be good for you, too. You never can tell when the call just might be the big break you have been seeking. Of course, the odds against that are long.

If you are a government worker, you have a particular duty to answer and return calls from citizens. In a broad sense the people are your employers, and you should treat them accordingly. No matter how inconvenient or inconsequential the call or caller may seem, the civil servant is obligated to return the call of every citizen, and to do it civilly.

Employees of private organizations do not have a constitutional obligation to return calls and talk nice, but they have to keep the best interests of their organization in mind. Whether making a product or providing a service, all private organizations depend on some group of clients or customers. There is no better way to offend an actual or potential customer than to be discourteous on the telephone or be impossible to reach.

Some people gain reputations for not returning calls. One famous midlevel eccentric bureaucrat I knew papered the inside of his office door with yellow call slips—unanswered. The wonder is that these people get work done at all and that anyone does business with them. These compulsive nonreturners like to pretend that they are too important and too busy doing great things to return a mere mortal's call. Actually, they come across to others as boors whose rudeness is a mark of their limited future.

Really great top-level officials always make certain that they return their calls. This is a mark of their greatness.

Want your calls returned? Return others' calls. It makes for better relationships.

## Rule 20: Get a Fax
The latest office status symbol is a fax machine. Get one. They are fabulous and can save lots of time and money. Other high-tech status symbols—speaker phones, voice mail, beepers, or

even cellular telephones—are merely child's play. The fax is the real thing.

The tremendous advantage of the fax is that it can send documents through the telephone. Since large organizations run on paper, it means that decentralized operations are finally feasible. In the past, even though deals were done over the telephone, some paper had to be transmitted to make it official, and this meant mail, messenger, or hand carrying it. Now, with the fax, the whole transaction can be done over the phone. Once a few wrinkles are worked out—like persuading payroll clerks to accept time cards and invoices sent over the fax as official—the entire way of doing business will be transformed.

There are some cautions about faxing. The most important is to restrain yourself from making puns from the name itself. Using "fax" as a transitive verb is fun the first twenty times you do it. Less erotic usages are not funny even the first time.

One result of the fax revolution is the explosion in the telephone numbers that attach to facsimile machines. Fax numbers are the newest and hottest item of office memorabilia. All true bureaucrats want to get as many other people's fax numbers as possible. These will be placed in your new special fax number list, and having someone's fax number will be the new sign of office intimacy. So you will have to collect your own set of fax numbers as an additional chore. On the other hand, you should be careful about giving out your fax number. There is apparently a big threat of junk faxes as advertisers and solicitors for all kinds of causes find out how to penetrate your electronic security shield. The advent of the fax age provides both promise and more work for conscientious office dwellers.

# Rule 21: Limit Personal Use of the Telephone

The telephone is the principal tool of the office. Without it government and commerce as we know them could not exist.

The telephone has been provided for official use. The XYZ Corporation or the government pays for the instrument, the wires, and the calls you make. They expect that you will use your business telephone strictly for business. They are wrong.

The telephone is used all the time for personal business. For the most part, this is necessary. People need to be able to inform spouses about working late, to turn the coffeemaker off, or whatever. Spouses need to be able to tell workers about plans, what needs to be picked up at the store on the way home, or about young Tom's braces. Similarly, reservations need to be made for lunch, squash courts, nail jobs, haircuts, and similar necessities. Finally, it is nice to be able to arrange social engagements and even chat briefly with friends, lovers, sweethearts, and others. So, the fact is that everyone uses business phones for personal business.

Every once in a while, some militant manager imposes a "no personal use" rule for the business telephones. Some organizations have even monitored calls to see which of the employees is using the phones for personal business. Some companies send phone bills to the guilty employees and demand payment. Punishments have been devised, posters placed, and pronouncements promulgated—all to no avail. The employee treats the phone as an extension of his or her psyche and uses it as necessary to function in the office environment.

You should exercise good sense when using a business telephone for personal affairs. The wise person limits his or her personal calls. There are only two basic rules:

1. Absolutely no personal long-distance calls charged to the corporation or Uncle Sam. Use your credit card, call collect, or wait until you get home. This is inexcusable.

2. Keep personal calls reasonably short. Don't spend all day making up with your sweetheart for last night's spat. Make a short apology and get on with official business.

If you exercise reason and restraint in your personal use of the business telephone, most bosses will be quite willing to allow you that privilege.

# Computers

The biggest high-tech office marvel is the computer. In the past ten years the computer has really developed from a large, expensive beast, kept in its own cage and operated only by specially trained people, to a small, relatively cheap tool found in every office and capable of being used by everyone. The computer promises to displace the telephone as the business tool par excellence, surpassed only by the combination of the telephone and the computer into huge networks of computers. The future of the computer is vast and the limits are uncertain, so it is wise to learn a few rules dealing with computers and how they will affect your work and your life.

## Rule 22: Learn How to Operate a Computer

Everyone should be able to operate a computer. They have become necessary in the exchange of information that is the essence of office work.

Many people have seen the light and have learned how to

operate computers. They appear on more and more desks, and the conversation at coffee breaks and even lunch turns more and more to software and real or imaginary problems with computers.

Operating a computer is really pretty easy. You just have to follow orders exactly. However, many computer types try to make it sound really hard, perhaps to boost their own ability. If it is hard and they can do it, they must be hot stuff. So there is still something of a cult atmosphere surrounding computer operators in many offices. They tend to talk in strange tongues and only to the initiated.

This tends to put off some other workers who are afraid to try to operate a computer. This is unfortunate. Employees who refuse to learn to operate a computer are shortchanging them-selves and their employers.

I believe that any officer worker can learn to operate a computer in a few hours if the matter is approached properly. I taught a course for government employees that depended in part on teaching retirement counselors how to use a model comparing benefits. Typically in our classes, half of the students had never operated a computer before. We had a computer for every two students and an interactive menu-driven program for the model. By the end of the first hour of instruction, every student was using the computer well and happily. We had broken through the fear of computers that still affects too many offices and too many employees.

I advise every worker to learn how to operate a computer. This often can be done through short courses offered by employ-ers. If you haven't got a computer on the job, try to get one. If you can afford it, buy one for your home. Not only can you learn about computer operation, but you might get some good out of home applications and have some fun, too. It extends your ability to work and it has an atmosphere all of its own.

Make no mistake, computers are here to stay and eventually they will be everywhere in offices. They are causing fundamental changes in the way business is conducted. Some are being felt now, but up to now we have mostly seen automation of manual routines. As we continue to apply computer-based logic to our work, its fundamental nature will change office work in ways we can only dimly perceive.

Above all, don't get uptight about operating a computer. It is no more difficult than operating a VCR or assembling a tricycle. And, if you have real trouble, you can always ask your children or grandchildren for help.

## Rule 23: Avoid Being a Computer Nut

It is important to know the difference between a computer operator and a computer nut. A computer operator uses a computer in his or her work; a computer nut loves computers.

My advice is to avoid being a computer nut. We need computer nuts—it is a dirty job and someone has to do it—but unless you really have a calling, let someone else do it.

There are degrees of computer nuts, depending on proficiency. At the lowest level of proficiency are the ones who know all about the latest models, programs, and peripherals. At the highest level of proficiency are the people who design and create computers. In between are the people who write software (programmers), people who figure out how to solve problems (systems analysts), and people who figure out how to lash it all together (systems integrators). These people are all legitimate computer nuts and live in a world of their own.

An apt comparison is perhaps to automobiles. Millions of us drive, but most do not design automobiles, make them, or even sell them. Most are only dimly aware of the way an automobile works. The thermodynamic cycle, the basis of the internal combustion engine, is remote. The interplay of engine and gears (do we still have gears?) is not well understood. Yet we operate automobiles fairly successfully for years and years. There are automobile nuts to whom a car is a way of life. Most of us tolerate these people and even admire them from afar. But most of us just want to get from Point A to Point B and find that a car is a convenient way to do that.

Most people are content to operate a computer. We don't

necessarily want to know how it works. We just want it to work.

The danger here is that the computer nuts want to make a mystique out of computers. They tend to complicate matters that already are overly complicated. There are so many terms and types and models that buying a computer system is worse than buying a new car. So there will be pressure for you to get involved in the details of computers. There will be pressure to compare exhaustively this program and that program and the latest hardware. There will be pressure to learn more than you care to know or need to know. There will be pressure for you to become a computer nut. Resist.

## Rule 24: Learn to Talk Like a Computer Nut

There is nothing that says that advice has to be consistent. In Rule 23 you were advised to avoid becoming a computer nut. Now I am advising you to learn to *talk* like a computer nut. This will provide protective coloration that will make life much easier.

Office life is intensely social. Certain things are common topics of conversation. Football is a favorite subject—the scores and players are big during coffee break on Monday mornings. There is the inevitable betting pool that appears mysteriously on Wednesday and Thursday. If there is a favorite team, the conversation is even more intense. So it helps to learn how to talk about football even if you don't really care about football. This is part of creating the image that you are "normal."

Football fans believe that the normal person *is* a football fan. They believe that anyone who does not like and learn about football is strange—a wimp, antisocial, perhaps, or even worse, an intellectual. There is nothing to be gained by making anti-football statements or by displaying ignorance of the game's fundamentals. Unless you are prepared to assume the role of office eccentric, you should feign some degree of knowledge of and interest in football. This can be done easily by merely scanning the sports section of the Sunday paper or listening to sports news. Pick up a few idioms from the football nuts and insert them carefully into your conversation at the office. Learn one sound bit of football news to use around the office. Something like, "The Redskins played well (or poorly) against the Cowboys yesterday" will suffice. If you don't go overboard, you can pass for a football fan enough to avoid being tagged as an eccentric.

The same approach applies, of course, to subjects such as baseball, bridge, gardening, music, and automobiles. A little protective coloration helps ease life in the office without having to make a big deal out of it.

In order to be able to talk like a computer nut, you should know some fundamental terms of computer lingo. The distinction between "hardware" and "software" is basic. If you are daring, you can refer to "vaporware," but be careful. Bits, bytes, bauds, and RAM and ROM sound nice and trip off the tongue very well. Learn the names of a few common software programs. Some ability to discuss the latest fashions in microchips, as in "Do you have a 286 or a 386 machine?" is impressive. It is also good to know the difference between a dot-matrix and a laser printer. Some mastery of printer-talk will allow you to speak of fonts and serifs as well. There is a large number of really interesting words in computer lingo. Some are old words with new meanings, and others are simply new words. Many of these words can be found in computer ads in the business section of your local newspaper. You might try reading the business section after you have finished the sports section.

You should never, ever disparage the computer nuts. Such epithets as "wire heads," "nerds," or even "computer nuts" should be avoided. Above all, never brag about being "computer illiterate." That is almost as bad as admitting that you did not watch the Super Bowl.

You can make it easier on yourself by learning just enough computer lingo to pass as a computer nut. And, if you do learn the lingo, there is a chance that you might learn something useful also.

# Work Habits

Your job is to get some work done. Despite the popular image of the office worker as slothful, uncaring, or both, I know that your Number One priority is to get your work done. Although each person's work differs somewhat, some rules apply across the board.

## Rule 25: Read the Laws and Regulations First

The first thing that you should do in a new job is to read all of the laws and regulations that pertain to it. This means federal, state, and local statutes, government or company policies, and the written regulations, standard operating procedures, and memorandums that create the basis for your work. It also means your own job or position description.

It is simply amazing the number of people who simply don't understand the basic framework of their jobs. Few take the time and trouble to learn the laws and regulations that define what they should do and what they can and cannot do.

Some workers learn parts of the laws. Some learn parts of the regulations. Mostly, these people are preparing memos for their bosses explaining some little bit here and another little bit there. But few people actually sit down and systematically read the laws or regulations or even read the documents sent down from higher management. Some don't even read their own job descriptions.

True, reading laws and regulations is a drag. These documents are not written for easy comprehension, and they are no fun. Moreover, it may be difficult even to get a copy of the laws and regulations pertaining to the job. Sometimes there is a dog-eared copy of an old regulation on the secretary's desk along with the phone directories. Sometimes not.

Another reason why this is seldom done is that there is simply not enough time to do it. When you arrive on the new job, there are instant demands for doing something and showing how smart you are. Many supervisors would not appreciate your retiring into your office for a week or so to read the laws and regulations.

Reading them on the bus or at home is possible but not easy. These are not light reading, and this would take a superhuman effort. Besides, this is part of the job and you should do it on the job.

Try reading these documents a little bit at a time. Maybe you could sneak in an hour's reading first thing in the morning before the meetings and phone calls and peremptory summonses to the front office preclude you from reading, or even thinking.

A thorough knowledge of the laws and regulations will not only help you do a better job but will also make you look good. Since most of your co-workers do not know the law, you could be the expert to whom others turn for advice.

Just one tip: Look out for the old hand in the office. There is always one or two others who have done their homework and have read the laws and regulations. This is often a senior employee who obtained his or her knowledge by osmosis over twenty-five years. Sometimes these people really know their stuff; sometimes they just have the reputation. If you do your homework, you will be able to tell which.

By the way, you can read up on the laws and regulations even if you are not reporting to a new job. Try it for the job you are on. It will help a lot.

## Rule 26: Keep Good Files

Information is power. History is power. Just knowing what happened is really power. The key to this power is keeping a good set of files.

You may have the naive notion that someone else—a clerk, perhaps—will be keeping the files. You may believe that all you have to do is like in the movies: "Miss Grant, bring me the McGregor file," and a vision of beauty will appear with a manila folder containing all of the information on the McGregor deal, organized, tabbed, and cross-indexed. Think again!

Filing in all organizations is uniformly poor. There is always insufficient clerical help to type, answer the phone, make coffee, make copies, and still have time for filing. At the working level, clerks spend most of their time just pounding on word processors. In the front office there are lots of clerks, but they only file administrative stuff like travel vouchers, pay slips, and agendas for past staff meetings. Nothing helpful is ever filed in the front office.

If you want good files, you will have to maintain them yourself. This is a real pain, but it is necessary if you are ever going to be able to look back at what happened and make sense of it. You will have to set up project files or functional files, and you will have to do the filing.

There is a great temptation to avoid filing. The papers pile up in your hold drawer or (if you are particularly inventive) in the "to-file box." You always mean to do the filing, but you never get around to it. Thus, when a memo on the McGregor deal has to be written in a hurry, you have to leaf through your hold drawer trying to find the documents on it. After a few frenzied stabs at this, you will recognize that filing is useful, even necessary.

Take the time to file properly. Set up files systematically. Make extra copies so that you can put one in each file folder. There are plenty of copiers around, and this is better than trying to remember or setting up a cross-reference system. Make tables of contents for each file drawer and even for the file folders themselves. This will save time when you have to find the critical document.

Computers have increased the need for good filing. They allow you to put a lot of information on little pieces of plastic called disks or diskettes. These come in two basic sizes: 5¼ inch and 3½ inch, though there are other sizes. Each diskette holds the equivalent of many pieces of paper—even a whole file drawer. So you can condense the space needed for storage, and that is a plus, but you still must set up a filing system for the diskettes. That will require an organized approach to naming your computer files, transferring them to diskettes periodically, labelling the diskettes, and storing them in some logical way. In some ways it is easier to browse through paper files than to scan a bunch of diskettes. So, computers will allow you to generate and store a lot more information in a smaller space, but it will require more discipline in filing, not less. This is particularly true if you want to or are required to keep a paper copy to back up each computer file.

The time invested in filing will be more than repaid by your ability to have information—and power—at your fingertips.

## Rule 27: Sit Down in Front

You will have to attend lots of meetings in auditoriums and large conference rooms. Some will be routine briefings on security, pay and benefits, and administrative trivia. Others will be more important and will relate directly to your job.

The behavior of people at large meetings is as fixed as the no-talking rule for Americans on elevators. Most sit in the middle of the room, but a large minority sits at the very back. Few people sit down in front, where the speaker can see them and talk to them easily.

There appears to be some cachet or prize for sitting in the back. It is as if a lack of interest in the subject is a mark of merit. Maybe the backbenchers want to appear disinterested; maybe they don't care about the way they come across. This indeed may be an element of the lackadaisical attitude that many office workers affect.

You can demonstrate interest and courtesy by sitting down in front. This will point you out as a person who cares and who doesn't mind showing that you care. Simply walking down to one of the front rows will give you a competitive edge over those who still skulk in the rear as if they were schoolchildren.

Sitting down in front helps the speaker and promotes interest in the group. I taught federal employees on their retirement systems in large groups. Habitually, these people would scatter toward the rear of the room. This made it hard to talk to them and it made it very hard to stimulate a group discussion. I used to tell them that they would not take the bad seats in the rear if they were paying for them. I have observed the same behavior among corporate employees.

In American schools the idea that it is good to hang back and bad to be eager sometimes permeates the atmosphere. This translates, among other things, into sitting in the back of the room. This is really a loser's attitude, and those who sit in the back also are playing games in other respects.

The best work is done by those who care and try. These are the people who, literally and figuratively, sit in the front of the room. If you want to be a better worker, you should adopt the attitude that you want to learn, want to hear, want to do good work, and that you sit in the front of the room.

# Rule 28: Make Memos for the Record Routinely

Memos for the record are a written record of a meeting, conversation, or other event. They are invaluable—a way to write the historical record, preserve the facts, and even sometimes to win the issue.

I remember one organization in which there were routine high-level meetings. The pachyderms would attend and thump their trunks on important matters and leave thinking they had done something. However, right after the meetings the administrative assistants would assemble to argue over who got to write the MFR. The assistants knew that it didn't matter nearly so much what actually happened in the meeting as what the MFR said happened.

The main reason for writing MFRs, however, is the fallibility of humans. Five people observing the same event will describe it differently. Two weeks later they will not be able to describe it at all. This phenomenon is not going to change. If office workers are to be able to treat the past as prologue, they need to have an agreed understanding of the past that hopefully is accurate as well.

The same assistants who vied for the right to write the MFR understood well that this document would also provide a basis for agreement. Six pachyderms can attend the same meeting, agree on a policy, and then depart, taking quite different versions of the policy. The MFR of the meeting allows for actual agreement, as opposed to ethereal agreement. This problem is well understood in commerce and is the basis for written contracts and the maxim, "Get it in writing!"

But even lesser events, such as phone calls and brown-bag luncheons, deserve MFRs if statements, facts, or agreements have been reached that should be preserved. It does not take much time to sit down and write a note to yourself. An MFR does not need to be fancy, and it may be handwritten or typed; it might be a file on a diskette. So be generous in your idea of what should be preserved. If in doubt, write it out.

When you have written your MFRs, you can put them in your subject files so that you will have a record at your fingertips.

## Rule 29: Use Your Friends to Get Things Done

Assuming that you want to get something done, it is perfectly proper to use your friends to do so. After all, what are friends for?

Recently, there have been sinister stories about corporate or government officials dealing with their friends. Everything is supposed to be done at arm's length. Calling on a friend to help get a paper through the front office or asking for friendly influence to obtain concurrence suddenly has become bad. It is as if it were better to do business with strangers or enemies.

Friendship is one of the lubricants that allows large organizations to function at all. For one thing it gives you priority for attention. If you have broken bread with another worker or swapped yarns over a couple of beers, your phone calls are more likely to be returned than if you are dealing with a stranger. Your ideas are likely to be heeded, although not necessarily approved more readily. Friendship does not give you automatic victory, but it guarantees a sympathetic hearing. That is important.

Once my office was fighting tooth and nail with an office in another agency over some turf and policy issues. The head of the other office—my counterpart—was reputed to be a man-eating tiger with a hearty appetite. After sitting through several meetings in which I was urged to declare war or worse, I thought it might be better to see for myself. I asked my project leader to set up a lunch for me and the tiger. In this instance my troops failed to carry out my request. Neither they nor the other guy's people were eager to have us meet. Maybe they thought we would harm each other physically. After weeks of stalling, I quietly called the other executive in his lair and invited him to lunch. We met at a downtown restaurant (no-man's land). We had three hours of delightful drinking, eating, and telling stories. This guy was no man-eating tiger, but he was no pussycat, either. He was a dedicated person with problems of his own, and we got along famously. Needless to say, we smoked the peace pipe and ended the war on agreeable terms. Thereafter, when friction arose, I knew that I could call him, get through, and settle the problems before our workers made them big. Because he was my friend, he could no longer be my enemy.

Whenever you have a tough problem, call on the people you know and trust to help you. They will be delighted to do so. They will also expect you to return the favor, so there is an obligation involved in this friendship business. Using friends is also called networking or reaching out. By any name it is a good way to get things done.

## Rule 30: Don't Use the Copier If You Can Avoid It

There is probably nothing more tedious than using a copying machine. Sure, the copier has changed the entire nature of office work and permitted the production and distribution of paper to an extent only barely dreamed of fifty years ago. Sure, the copier is an indispensable element in the new system that facilitates reworking papers and reworking them until stopped by deadlines or sheer exhaustion. Sure, the copies have to be made. But the process is boring.

So my advice is to avoid using the copier. Try to get someone else to make the copies for you. If you are a big boss, there is no problem. Simply tell your Dragon that you need X copies. The Dragon will order a minion to do the dirty work, since Dragons consider copying beneath them. If you are a boss, the same thing applies, but the secretary will be making the copies for you. If you are just a plain worker, avoiding the copier demands real ingenuity.

You can try the straightforward approach, but chances are it won't work. That is to ask the administrative assistant or secretary to make the copies. The problem is that these people are so busy typing or word processing and answering the phones that they will be reluctant to use the copier, or at least will plead overwork to avoid it. The branch chief is likely to back up the secretary because the typing load always exceeds the typing capability, and there are always papers that are late or due the next morning. So getting copying done by asking the proper person is probably futile.

In some fortunate organizations there is an entry-level person who has ill-defined duties but who tidies up and performs errands. This person is available to do your copying for you, but not well and not in a hurry. If you ask the office gofer to make 100 copies by tomorrow morning, you are just as likely to get 20 copies next week. After a few of these experiences, you will learn that copying, like politics, is the art of the possible.

So you really have to try to get a co-worker to do it for you. This is hard because everyone dislikes copying and tries to avoid it. One method is the Tom Sawyer ploy. This involves demonstrating such complete incompetence at using the copier that others do it for you out of pity or to prevent you from screwing up the machine again. Feigning incompetence in the copying room may give you a reputation as a general klutz that could impair promotions and bonuses. Still, it might be worth it.

It is likely that everyone will be avoiding the copier. For one thing, everyone will have read this book, so you will probably have to make your own copies, just like almost everyone else. If this is the case, you should do it quickly, competently, and casually, because all of the other people will be in line behind you waiting to make copies.

## Rule 31: Don't Use the Copier for Personal Business

The copier is an attractive nuisance, like a swimming pool or backyard rope swing. That is, it attracts malfeasance by its very nature. The opportunity to copy personal items on the office machine is apparent to all, and too many workers do this and thereby commit a crime. In fact, the only time that workers are eager to use the machine is when their personal stuff needs to be copied.

I have seen people copying civic association and PTA notices, and even party invitations, on the office machine. The weekly football and baseball pools also are produced on the office copier. Some people even copy their personal business and tax records on the office machine.

This is no small matter. It costs from four to ten cents per copy on a machine, so the amount of corporation or government money wasted in this way adds up to quite a sum in a typical fiscal year.

Bosses try to prevent this crime. They inveigh against the practice at staff meetings, put out policy papers, attach stern warnings to the copiers, and even load in special paper bearing a notice like, "reproduced at government expense." None of this deters the determined copier crook.

Next to misappropriation of government pens (a major pastime in the Washington, D.C., area, where every gas station attendant has one), the use of copiers for personal business is the most prevalent crime committed routinely by government employees. This is also true for private companies, except that because they have to pay for the illicit copies out of the bottom line, corporations tend to be more ingenious, putting cypher locks and other controls on their copiers. Nevertheless, the problem is there for the private sector.

The answer to this has to be a simple slogan—something original, like "Just say no." For the only way that this practice will stop is if office workers stop it. My advice to you is to avoid using the office machine for personal business. Libraries and post offices have cheap coin-operated copiers. There are numerous copying shops where you can get the PTA notices reproduced. Finally, the cost of personal copiers has dropped to where many people can afford to have one at home. So there is no excuse for this crime, other than sheer greed and lack of caring about the shareholders' or taxpayers' dollars.

## Rule 32: Wait for Help before Doing It Yourself

At some stage in your work life you will run into a situation in which you don't really know what to do. You will have to accomplish a goal and you won't have the knowledge or skills needed to do it.

The natural instinct is to ask for help. You work in a vast organization that is designed, among other things, to provide you the knowledge and skills to help you do your work. If you need computer support, you go to the computer shop. If you need audiovisual support, you go to the audiovisual shop. If you need other help, you go to the appropriate place in your organization. This is normal and natural. It is also good policy.

The first place to go is your boss. The boss gets paid to help you do your work. This may come as a surprise to the boss, who may believe that you are there to help *him*. Actually, it works both ways. If you are stumped, see the boss and ask how to proceed.

Most bosses will oblige. They seldom leap in and do the work themselves, but they have been around a while and know whom to call and what to do. They know a person in the computer shop. They know how to get slides made quickly for a briefing. They know how to get help from within their own organization and from other organizations. One of the reasons that they are bosses is because they know these things. Take advantage of their experience and wisdom when you need them.

Then you should wait for the help to arrive before crashing on into the thicket. There is no point in doing an amateurish job when professionals can do it so much better and faster. So lay out your plan, place your requests for help, and sit tight. That will provide a better product in the long run and it will be a tribute to your own organizational skills.

The advantage of a team is that everyone plays his or her position and does what he or she does best. While this ideal is not always achieved, there is enough truth in it to make it work for you. The key is planning and lead time. You should understand your limitations and ask for help enough in advance to bring the product in on time anyway.

Don't try to do it all yourself. Be patient. Let the organization function as it is designed to function.

## Rule 33: Do It Yourself without Waiting for Help

On the other hand, there are times *not* to wait for help. You must push ahead against all odds and do it yourself.

An organization does not always respond well or quickly to requests for help. Each professional has lots of work to do without your additional workload. The computer people always have machines and programs to fiddle with. The audiovisual people always seem to be doing something. So when you ask for help, particularly in a hurry, sometimes you will find that you just don't get much response. You will get halfhearted assurances and vague promises. You will get no great feeling of relief.

Sometimes when you ask the boss for help, you will not get it. This depends on the kind of boss you have. Some don't want to help. Even good bosses get overloaded or fight with the spouse at breakfast, and at times their answer may be a surly rebuff. Don't take this personally, for even bosses who have not had a domestic quarrel think that you are there to solve problems rather than cause them.

So waiting for help may not be the best thing to do sometimes. Even if you have created a great plan and allowed lots of time, the help you have requested may come in late or not at all. Suppose that you have been tasked with putting together a large report on the activities of your office. In true collegial manner, you have prepared an outline, established targets for the number of pages for each section of the outline, and assigned the sections to the various divisions with a deadline for their drafts. The deadline arrives, and only half of the divisions have responded. You call the late divisions and ask for their drafts. They stall. Your boss is asking where the draft of the report is. What do you do? One possibility is to go to your boss and blame the delay on the divisions that are late. This would be accurate but would be unlikely to satisfy the boss. Another possibility would be for you to draft the sections for the missing divisions and include them in your draft report. This is a lot of extra work, but it has several things going for it. You will get the attention of the late divisions, for they will not like someone else writing up their projects. They will respond with detailed comments on your draft, even though they could not provide a draft themselves. More important, by refusing to wait for help, you will have gotten the job done on time and have satisfied your boss.

Another consideration is that when someone else does something for you, you never get quite the same product that you would have produced yourself. You know exactly what you want and you care intensely about the product. So you devote loving care to a task that to an outsider may be nothing more than just a chore in a day filled with chores. There is a possibility that help might not give you the high-quality product you seek. If quality is not the issue, it might not establish the nuances you intend.

There are circumstances in which it is better to do something by yourself rather than wait for help. Perhaps time pressure is intense or there is a good chance that help will be late, insincere, or inadequate. Maybe you have a great stake in the project. If you really love it and have confidence in yourself, go ahead. Take a chance. Don't wait for help.

# Meetings

It seems that office life consists of meetings punctuated by lunch and coffee breaks. There are staff meetings, team meetings, sales meetings, project meetings, proposal meetings, interagency meetings, program meetings, and meeting meetings.

Most people profess to hate meetings. They complain, calling them a waste of time. They seem reluctant to go to meetings. They even try to avoid them.

This is a sham. People love meetings. They provide structure to an unstructured environment. Unless a worker actually has routine paperwork to do, there is little routine, measurable work for midlevel office employees. The work that they should do involves policy formulation, program analysis, and other soft and mushy kinds of things. This leaves most office workers wondering what to do once the survival-type work is done. Meetings solve the problem of how to occupy time.

Meetings supply all kinds of good things. They provide an opportunity to mingle and hear interesting things. They help measure the importance of the worker. They provide an occasion for camaraderie, even socializing. They even get some useful work done once in a while.

Actually, meetings are vital to the working of any organization. Many modern corporations are so vast and interconnected that an extensive network of vertical and lateral communications is required to keep information flowing. This is certainly true of the federal government. So meetings, despite the kidding about them (and I have just done some of that!) are important communication events. I like meetings and believe that, properly conducted, they are of great benefit.

If one is to be a better officer worker, it is necessary to deal with meetings and perform at and benefit from them. The next set of rules is designed to improve your meeting behavior.

## Rule 34: Your Place or Mine?

One of the petty but perplexing problems is where to have the meeting. This is the office equivalent of "your place or mine?" There are some rules that tend to mitigate the rancor arising from this simple choice.

The general rule is that the junior person visits the office of the higher-ranking person. Deputy assistant secretaries visit assistant secretaries, not the other way around. The project manager visits the vice president. This has a little to do with convenience and a lot to do with status, but there has to be strong rationale for violating this rule.

If you are calling or sponsoring a meeting of people from several groups, you are generally obligated to be the host. You are expected to provide a room and paraphernalia to conduct the business.

Problems occur mostly between peers or when the difference in status is small or a matter of dispute. Some people make a point of insisting that others visit them. They may do this to inflate their own importance or diminish the status of the visitors. If two such people try to arrange a meeting, it can get pretty nasty quickly, and the issue of whose place transcends the topic that was the reason for the meeting.

My advice is to go to the other person's office when you are visiting peers. This eliminates a fight over status and allows you to be generous with your time and energy. Since you are doing the travelling and thus consuming time that could otherwise be used for writing memos, this will require an effort. Your sacrifice may or may not be noticed, but you will be right.

Of course, you may have legitimate reasons for wanting to have the meeting at your place. Your schedule may be tight, the documents are too bulky to carry conveniently, or it is your turn. In this event simply approach the person you want to meet with and negotiate the location honestly. If you meet with this person frequently, you can institute an informal system of taking turns. If you plan to visit a stranger, you should go to his or her office for the first visit if the meeting is your initiative. If there is any difficulty over location, give in at once without a murmur.

Another reason to visit others in their offices is to see what that person's environment is like. People tend to reflect their environment. There is nothing like a personal reconnaissance to give you a feel for the values and tribal culture shown by the other person's office. Though offices tend to be similar, an experienced person can tell a lot about an agency and an individual from the layout and decor of his or her office and desktop. So go to the other person's office and learn something.

Courtesy is simply good form. Going out of your way to visit others in their offices is courteous and also educational.

## Rule 35: Be Hospitable

If you are having visitors to your office or agency for a meeting, be hospitable. They are human beings and should be extended the courtesy afforded guests.

The visitors should be greeted when they arrive and not left to stew in corridors, at the receptionist's desk, or at guard posts. The host is responsible for arranging easy entry and escorting the visitors into the meeting room.

The host should start the meeting promptly. The visitors have already spent time in travel, and they should not have to wait around while the host finishes up other business. Starting on time is courteous.

The host should offer coffee, tea, or soft drinks. Even if the visitors decline, the offer tends to warm the atmosphere, making conditions more conducive to a good meeting. Also, visitors may be anxious about your meeting. Having a cup of coffee or tea to hold and sip tends to put them at ease.

If your office cannot offer refreshments, don't mention that; just ignore the whole thing. But an office without coffee or tea does not seem efficient, so you have already started on the wrong foot. In offering coffee or tea, be reasonably efficient. Don't seem clumsy and don't apologize. Take the trouble to find out where the Styrofoam cups are as part of preparing for the meeting. It is tacky to complicate such a simple thing by rifling several filing cabinets and desks, only to end up offering an unwashed mug belonging to an absent worker. Provide refreshments efficiently and unobtrusively to set a good scene for the meeting.

As host you are also obligated to run a reasonable meeting and end on time. This is covered in another rule, but it applies as part of hospitality as well as good business.

Doing business in the office is aided by civility, eased by courtesy, and warmed by hospitality. As in so many other matters, treat your guests as you would like to be treated.

## Rule 36: Have an Agenda

Communication experts give a lot of advice about how to conduct meetings. I am not going to go over all of that, but there is one rule that is absolute if a meeting is going to be more than a bull session.

Every meeting should have an agenda. An agenda is a plan of what the meeting is to do. It helps the chairperson keep the work moving and provides assurance that work will be done. I made a point of preparing a written agenda for every meeting for which I was responsible, either as chairperson or as project officer. When you are setting up a meeting for your boss to chair, you should prepare the agenda and check it with him in advance.

Most people go to meetings unprepared. Written material provided days in advance often is ignored until just before the meeting, when the attendee grabs it up in haste to read on the subway en route. So don't count on any of the attendees knowing what to do. Actually, many people approach meetings like they go to movies—they expect to be entertained. If there is no structure, they tend to sit around and sulk or, even worse, to get mean and start complaining. I have attended meetings where there was no agenda; these generally turned out to be disasters in which reputations were tarnished and valuable programs trashed. On the other hand, I have seen meetings where no one could possibly have known anything on the subject turn into masterpieces of cogent group therapy—all because there was an agenda. An office worker's mind works best when focusing on written words. Having a few numbered sentences provides a beacon through the thickets of thought.

Lack of preparation for a meeting is poor but tolerable on the part of the attendees, but it is inexcusable on the part of the chairperson.

A written agenda has a marvelous effect. It certainly makes the job of chairing the meeting easier. He or she has only to say, "Let's discuss the first item on the agenda," and the meeting is started. Then, after the discussion on that item dwindles to incoherence or provokes an argument, the chairperson can regain control by declaring victory over the first item and moving on to Number Two. It helps if some thought has gone into the agenda, such as listing items in some logical priority or order. But a good agenda is not really necessary. Having one is.

So you should always prepare an agenda to hand out to every person at a meeting for which you are responsible. Simply writing it out will force you to focus on the purpose of the meeting and how to meet it. During the meeting the agenda will structure the event and will help you get something done.

You will be surprised at the added influence the simple device of an agenda will provide. The second law of thermodynamics says that order tends to become disorder unless energy is expended to restore order. When applied to the office, this law means that disorganization will ultimately take over unless workers do something positive. Adequate preparation for a meeting will provide some energy to fight the relentless trend toward disorganization.

## Rule 37: Have a Paper to Table

You should always prepare some document when you attend a meeting. It does not matter whether you are having an informal discussion with your boss, a staff meeting of your team, or a session with the board of directors of your company.

The advantage goes to the person who has prepared for the meeting. This simple truth seems to escape most people. You have probably noticed that most people just get up from their desks to go into a meeting without even thinking about the subject in advance. Sometimes a good chairperson will prepare an agenda and, of course, when formal presentations have been scheduled, there is much work done in preparing them. But most of the impromptu meetings that occupy so much time take place without preparation.

This leads to a situation in which people sit around mumbling about what to do. This occurs most often in meetings among peers. If a supervisor meets with subordinates, there is likely to be a directed session, which may or may not make sense.

You will recall that the one-eyed man is king in the land of the blind. The same thing is true in the office. The person who prepares for the meeting will dominate it and may win his points.

I recommend that you spend the short time it takes to prepare a point paper, an agenda, or a fact sheet to bring to a meeting. You should have enough copies for each person there.

When everyone starts to hem and haw, place your handout on the table. This will provide an instant focus. Others will seize on your paper like a drowning man clings to a life raft. They will start using your paper as the agenda.

This makes you look good. The others may be grateful to you for saving a potential waste of time. Also, since you have set the agenda, you will be in a great position to win your points or at least to establish the tone and content of the discussion.

It may be inadvisable to present your paper at every meeting. Sometimes the chairman is prepared. Sometimes the climate is not right. You may wish to keep the paper in your briefcase. Still, you should always be prepared to offer a concrete document at each meeting.

## Rule 38: Don't Exceed Your Allotted Time

An office has two different approaches to time. On one hand, there is never enough time to do it right. On the other hand, there is always time to do it over.

Actually, time is scarce for managers and executives. The higher one goes in the hierarchy, the more precious time becomes. Vice presidents and assistant secretaries do not even manage their own time. A Dragon guards the gates of the inner sanctum and manages the appointments, meetings, and work of the Great Person. The executive is given one or more little cards upon which is the daily schedule. Most of the time the executive merely does what he or she is told, for breaking the schedule creates havoc among the lesser lights waiting in anterooms or "on call" in their own offices.

One of the prerogatives of high position is to disrupt the schedules of underlings. When a higher boss has a brainstorm and calls an unscheduled meeting, there is a cascade of broken appointments, time lost in waiting around, and work undone. This is not one of the prerogatives of subordinates.

One of the worst sins is to run overtime. You have a duty to keep to your assigned time for a meeting, briefing, office visit, or anything else that requires the presence or attention of your boss. This is true whether or not the boss manages time well. If he or she meanders, you still must get in and get out on time. For this, you will gain many points from the Great Person's Dragon.

One of the top officials in the White House gained his enviable reputation solely on his ability to end a meeting on time.

This person knew nothing about the meetings over which he presided, but he had a good watch and a keen sense of propriety. Thus, he ended each meeting on the dot, no matter what was happening. Since this forced the workers to achieve a certain discipline, it may have been a great technique, though the benefits were inadvertent.

My advice is to plan carefully for a communications event with your boss or co-workers. Estimate the time required and try to have that amount of time put into the schedule. Then prepare to occupy that time gainfully. Always leave some time for questions and discussion, prepare material to be thrown in if there is an embarrassing pause, and prepare clues to end the meeting for bosses who hesitate to close. Even be prepared to end early if you cover the material faster than you thought. Bosses love extra minutes; they are just like finding money on the sidewalk.

Never, ever run over your allotted time. If you do this, the boss will turn surly and you will endanger your points. It is better to accept partial victory by trimming the agenda than to risk complete defeat by going on too long. I have seen people turn certain victory into defeat simply by not knowing when to stop talking. Your boss has to consume great amounts of disparate data during a normal day, and he or she has to stick to his or her schedule to do this. Help your boss by planning and exercising your discipline in using his or her time wisely.

## Rule 39: Learn to Brief

The briefing is perhaps the epitome of modern office practice. A briefing is a short oral presentation—hence the name. It has developed over the years into an art form of elegance and power. Unfortunately, it is better in concept than in reality. So easy to do; so hard to get done.

You should learn to brief. You will have to do this often in your career. You will brief bosses, meetings, big bosses, big meetings, and groups of friends, strangers, and enemies.

Incidentally, briefings are oral presentations *and* verbal presentations. Oral refers to the spoken word; verbal implies the use of language. Even though Webster's is wishy-washy on this matter, I adhere strictly to "oral" when talking about spoken communications. You may do otherwise, but you will be incorrect.

The key point about a briefing is that it is intended to be brief. You are supposed to convey a certain amount of information in a limited amount of time. This requires a high degree of organization and a lot of work. Simply standing up and blatting out all you know about Subject A is not giving a briefing.

I have attended thousands of briefings and have given a few. Most were pretty good. Some were really bad. Bad means long, disjointed, and with poor graphic aids.

Unless you are trying to kill an idea by obscuring it, try to make your briefings clear and to the point. First, find out how much time you have. Then find out how much you have to say. Compare the two. Then reduce the subject matter to fit the time available. Do this ruthlessly. If you are briefing some bosses, allow lots of time for interruption and questions. Then lay the main points out in an outline and use that to organize your presentation.

Most briefings use some kind of visual aid—a chart or table projected on a screen displaying data or concepts in the form of bullets. Bullets are short phrases that imply an entire idea. Sometimes you can use short sentences, which present a complete idea. The bullets focus on the main points and are handy refreshers for the presenter on what to say. Many briefings use transparencies or viewgraphs and an overhead projector. It is possible also to use 35mm slides. The technology for making these is much better now than a few years ago. If you use them properly, slides will help organize the briefing, assist in the presentation, and later serve as reminders of the briefing. See Rule 40 on how to use briefing slides properly.

This brings up a crucial issue: Is it better to hand out photocopies of the slides before the oral presentation or afterward? Proponents of the former believe that this helps recipients follow the briefing and provides a handy place to take notes. Proponents of handing the copies out afterward believe that having the slides during the briefing detracts from the oral presentation and leads overeager recipients to look ahead and lose concentration. I side with the latter group. I never hand out copies of slides in advance if I can help it. I always have copies of my slides to give people afterwards.

Briefing is a very important communication skill. Grab every opportunity to brief. Keep it simple, keep it short, and use slides. You will do a good job.

## Rule 40: Use Briefing Slides Properly

This rule pertains to overhead projector transparencies and 35mm slides used in oral briefings. The previous rule discussed the basics of briefings; this rule dwells on the slides themselves. The main points for the proper use of slides are as follows:

1. Put only four or five ideas (bullets) on a slide.
2. Discuss every bullet.
3. Use readable print.
4. Allow two minutes per slide for discussion.
5. Take the slide off when you are finished with it.

There is a limit to the amount of information a human can absorb from a slide. This means you should limit the data you put on a slide. Unfortunately, this rule is often ignored. I have seen slides covered from top to bottom. The unfortunate briefer often compounds the error by apologizing for his incomprehensible slide as being a bit "busy." There is no need for that; the audience knows the slide is too full of data to be useful. A "busy" slide indicates that the briefer was too lazy to prepare properly. If you are using the bullet technique, use only four or five ideas or topics per slide. You might get up to six or seven if they all tie together. But in the slide business, less is more.

Discuss every bullet on every slide. Don't throw up a list of twenty important factors and talk about two. That really upsets the audience, which wonders what is not being told. The mystery bullets are like static that makes it hard to hear the message.

Make certain that even that old guy in the back can read the slide. Use big print. Never copy a page from a document or book and throw it up on a screen. Above all, never do this and then comment on how the slide is "probably too small for you to see," and then read the text to the audience. This is one of the worst briefing blunders, but it is done more often than I care to contemplate. Use common sense and large type.

You will probably spend one to two minutes on each slide. If you are spending more, break up the ideas. I like to show the bullets and then discuss each with the audience in more detail. Each bullet triggers or cues the discussion. It also reminds the viewers when they get the hard copy later. A mortal briefing sin is to read the bullets verbatim. Don't do that. Ever.

Another big mistake is to leave a slide on while discoursing on another topic. When you have finished with the slide, shut it off. If you are not going to show another slide immediately, shut the machine off. It is hard enough to get your points across without having the recipients staring at the last slide wondering what it meant or being dazed by the glare from the light on the empty screen. If you are going to talk without a slide, do that.

Slides are a big help in communicating your ideas during a briefing. They need to be well constructed and used appropriately. This is so easy that I wonder why so many briefers do it poorly.

## Rule 41: Take the Worker to the Big Meeting

The work is done. George or Marie has finished the paper, and you are about to attend the Big Meeting of all of the bosses to discuss the subject.

If you can, take George or Marie along with you to the meeting so they can see the bosses talking about the work that they did.

Too often, midlevel managers or, particularly, senior managers take going to high-level meetings for granted. Visiting the assistant secretary's office or the corporate offices is no big deal to them, for they go there often. However, the poor worker bee who did the job may not go there very much and may not have even been in the big boss's office.

I remember attending a meeting at the Old Executive Office Building with some big wheels. I had been there often, but it was still a thrill to have to clear White House security and go into that grand old building. When I got back, I told Marie what had happened and she said somewhat wistfully that she would like to attend a meeting there sometime. I realized that some of the psychic reward from government service is in going to important places. The same thing is undoubtedly true in the private sector.

People who go to important places routinely lose their awe, at least somewhat, and may fail to realize that their subordinates would love to go to the White House, the company president's office, or even the front office next higher up.

Some managers may view their access to Big Meetings and important places as feathers in their own caps not suitable for the peons who work for them. They believe that allowing the worker to attend somehow diminishes their own importance. This is a sad attitude.

Most managers probably never even consider that the peons might like to attend the Big Meeting, forgetting how they themselves hankered to attend when they were not so big and important.

Some big wheels restrict attendance for space limitations, security, or just not liking crowds. You may not be able to take your worker bee along, but if there is a chance from time to time, reward the person who does the work by taking them to the Big Meeting.

# Socializing at the Office

Since much of your life is spent at the office—working or not working—you must realize that the social aspects of your job are very important, not only to you as an individual but to the group. For most office workers the office and people in the office, or the people they meet through the office, are a big part of their social life. For some workers the office is the most important element of their social life, or maybe the only element in their social life. If you are to be regarded as a member of the group, learn how to participate in the office social life. You may choose not to participate, but you will be in a better position if you play your part in office socializing.

These are some rules to help you make the grade socially at the office. They are not the only rules, but they will give you an idea. Actually, socializing at the office is much the same as socializing anywhere. Just be yourself, relax, and have a good time—carefully.

# Rule 42: Remember First Names

The language you speak and write at work is most likely to be Standard American Office Worker. While some regional dialect is permitted, the Standard American syntax and word usage is basic. As part of the overall speech habits in your culture, the use of first names is customary.

It is the American thing to use first names. We make a fetish of it. The use of first names in other societies is much more restricted. In some societies the honorifics, such as "mister" or "honored," are used even among family members. In our society we use the honorifics only on ceremonial occasions, in situations with a wide disparity in rank, and sometimes even to express disdain for the target. We like to get on a first-name basis right away; this goes for the office as well.

The basic reason to address co-workers or subordinates by their first names is simple friendliness. Using a first name is the nice thing to do. It establishes an informal and easy relationship right away. This puts a premium on learning and using the first names of your co-workers. It is a sign of ignorance or apathy to address a fellow worker by the last name, unless you are fighting with or really dislike him or her. It is a sign of camaraderie and belonging to use a first name.

The situation gets complicated when addressing either a superior or a subordinate. In a hierarchy, addressing someone by his or her first name does not necessarily mean intimacy or even friendship. It often is a facade, but an important facade. It gives the illusion of equality without the substance and, by fostering the illusion, increases the permissible degree of difference between superiors and subordinates. After all, the worker can at least feel the equal of the boss he calls by the first name in private.

If you are a boss, you will have to judge whether you are comfortable using the first names of your workers. In some cases your familiarity will be taken as an invitation to similar familiarity, and we all know that familiarity is alleged to breed contempt.

So you should recognize that it may not be simple friendship when the boss calls you by your first name. Addressing servants and slaves familiarly has been the masters' prerogative throughout the centuries. The cachet is in doing it upward.

The major point of using first names, however, is not class struggle but friendship. My advice is to use first names regularly with your fellow workers—peers, subordinates, and the boss, if that is encouraged in private.

## Rule 43: Don't Call Your Boss by the First Name

Like all general rules, the one that encourages you to call others by their first names has an exception, which is how you address your boss. The rule here is never to use the boss's first name at official public occasions.

The purpose of this exception to the general rule is to promote the effectiveness and status of the boss, who, after all, is the tribal chief.

The occasions for more formal address are meetings, conferences, luncheons, and dinners. When addressing or referring to your boss at these affairs, you should use Miss, Ms., Mrs., Mr., Doctor, Colonel, General, or Honorable.

The degree of intimacy or friendship you share with the boss has nothing to do with this. Even if you were his college roommate, best man at his wedding, godfather to his daughter, and spent last night carousing together, it is still proper to use the formal form of address for your boss in public. In fact, the more intimate your relationship, the more powerful will be the formal form of address when you use it. The fact that you, a known pal, are deferential in public will really increase regard for your boss. I can tell you that he or she will appreciate it.

Some bosses insist on being called by their honorifics all of the time. Don't worry about these, for they don't understand how to be a boss. The boss who is really respected and liked will be addressed by his or her first name inside the tribe but will be addressed formally in front of outsiders. These are both signs of respect.

There are some new kids and a few old hands who think that calling the boss by the first name in public ostentatiously will demonstrate their clout. Nothing could be farther from the truth. This only illustrates a vast lack of understanding of tribal culture.

The best rule is this: If in doubt, use the formal title. This can never hurt, and if the boss wants you to call him or her by the first name, he or she will tell you.

# Rule 44: Attend Office Parties

Another aspect of the tribal culture is the ritual office party. These occur on special occasions such as birthdays, retirements, farewells, and Christmas. Parties are an important part of the tribal culture and you should always attend. If you are the boss, it is particularly important that you attend all tribal rituals, for you are the chief.

True, many of these parties are not great fun, but that is beside the point. They are part of the social activities of the office. Office workers seldom socialize with each other outside of work except on these ritual occasions. I don't know why, but I suspect it has to do with trying to maintain some independence from the office tribe. Another reason may be a desire to do what one wants to do in nonwork hours without having to conform to the tribal culture of the office. At any rate, office parties are powerful rituals, and there is even a set of rules for them.

Luncheons are preferred for most retirements and farewells, except for big bosses, who are honored with a dinner. Luncheons provide an opportunity for the entire tribe to travel to a restaurant, break bread, share some soothing potion (perhaps even getting tipsy), and engage in the mumbo jumbo of testimonials and speeches. This forges firmer bonds for the group. It does nothing for the person who is retiring or being transferred because he or she is no longer going to be in the group, except as emeritus. These parties are not for the person who is leaving; they are for those who are staying.

The birthday party is another entire class of ritual. This is normally done during office hours and seldom rates a luncheon. Instead, a cake is provided and coffee, punch, or sometimes harder stuff is set up, and the tribe stands or sits around an office or conference room making desultory small talk. There is always the ritual singing of "Happy Birthday." There are always the jokes about age and other sallies at the birthday boy or girl. There may be a speech by the honored guest, unless he or she giggles out of it. Then the party breaks up informally as the members of the group drift back to their routines. Oh, yes, there are always the telephone calls that have to be answered, usually by the newest clerk, during the party. While trite and predictable, birthday parties are an essential ritual. The only thing worse than having to attend other people's birthday parties is to have your own birthday forgotten.

The big parties are the most ritualistic and the most fun. These are the Christmas party and those sponsored by the tribe's front office. There has been a lot written about the perils of Christmas parties, so I am not going to repeat all of that stuff here. Suffice it to say that caution is advisable and attendance is mandatory. You might even have a good time.

I have had a ball at some Christmas parties given by competing tribes. In one large organization the tribal chiefs competed with one another on the splendor of their Christmas parties. This is somewhat like the northwestern Indians who gained status by giving away their possessions. The more one gave away, the more status they accrued. Well, one year this whole thing got out of hand as each office vied to provide more and better food and drink. It is a wonder that any of us survived without becoming fat alcoholics. The final party served—this is true—champagne and caviar!

Office parties are what you make of them. They are important and can be relaxing occasions for good fellowship. It is good sometimes to learn about the real human beings behind the facade of typist, program analyst, engineer, salesperson, or computer operator. It **is a** particularly good time for the tribal elders to get to know the neophytes and pass on some tribal lore, so go and have a good time at office parties.

# Rule 45: Don't Get Drunk in Front of the Boss

This is simple. Don't ever drink so much alcohol that you appear to your boss to be drunk.

There will be many opportunities in an office to get drunk. There is less emphasis on drinking than before and the new trend is toward beer and wine instead of the hard stuff. But you can still get drunk on beer or wine.

There will be office and Christmas parties, social affairs at various homes, luncheons, dinners, and official functions. Alcoholic beverages will be served at most of these, and the possibility of drinking too much will always be there. Don't do it.

This is not a plea for abstinence or even a general admonition about getting drunk. Obviously, it is good policy not to drink too much at any time. It is bad policy to drink if you are driving. It's much better not to get drunk at all.

But if you insist on getting drunk, do it in front of your spouse and kids, in front of your minister or lawyer, or even in front of your friends or co-workers. Never get drunk in front of your boss.

If you get drunk and make a fool of yourself, you will not amuse the boss. He is interested somewhat in you as a human being, but he is interested primarily in you as an effective member of his working team. His future rests on you just as much as yours rests on him. Almost all bosses object to having their promotions depend on a drunken bum.

Getting drunk in front of the boss is an indication of poor judgment and lack of self-control and will get you bad ratings and cost you promotions and key assignments. Good judgment and self-control are valued highly by bosses.

Now, there is nothing to prevent you from being convivial or happy or even lighthearted after a glass or two of wine or some beers. Parties are thought to be improved by a moderate level of alcoholic intake that dampens inhibitions and promotes camaraderie. This may or may not be true, but a little drinking is tolerated. A lot of drinking is not. So exercise judgment and self-control by cutting yourself off before you get drunk, make a fool or a beast of yourself, and injure your career drastically.

The one situation that is worse than being drunk in front of the boss is when the boss is drunk in front of you. All bosses have human weaknesses. This extends to all sorts of bad behavior, from sexual harassment to dictatorial demands. One proverbial weakness of bosses is overdrinking, so it is possible that you may be at a party at which the boss is making a fool of himself or herself. If this happens, get out quickly.

The boss might forgive you for being drunk even if it slows you down a few years. The boss is not likely to forgive you for observing him or her in a moment of supreme idiocy. People just don't like to be seen when they are out of control, and no matter how jovial the manner, the drunken boss is a dangerous animal.

If you are so unfortunate as to have a drunkard for a boss, try to avoid situations that will put you in the position of seeing him or her drunk. While you still must participate in the social life of the group, you might be able to leave early or stay out of the way.

If you cannot get away, you can treat the boss's drunken behavior with neither approbation nor disdain. Just be cool and avoid him or her. Remember, a drunken boss is not likely to survive long, particularly if he or she gets drunk often in front of the Big Boss.

## Rule 46: Join the Coffee Club

One of the most troubling issues for any organization is the coffee club. Coffee appears to be the elixir of life for office workers. Though there are a few elitists or cultists who drink tea, coffee is the prevalent beverage. Walk into any well-organized office and you will see an automatic coffeemaker, a metal can of coffee, and possibly some creamer, artificial sweetener, and even sugar.

The problem with this is that coffee does not make itself. Left on its own, it creates a great mess. Therefore, there has to be some system for buying provisions, making coffee, and cleaning up the mess.

Buying provisions is the duty of the coffee club manager, which is discussed in Rule 47. The real problems are in who makes the coffee and cleans up.

In the good old days there was no problem. The secretaries made the coffee and the rest of the workers drank it. That delightful custom has largely disappeared with the emancipation of secretaries from personal service. It is true that in front offices, secretaries still make the coffee and will even serve it—at least for important visitors. This kind of treatment, however, is generally restricted to vice presidents, assistant secretaries, and other big bosses. Even some senior executives nowadays have to make coffee. Whether this is efficient use of highly paid time is beside the point. Coffee is a social issue.

That is why everyone should join the coffee club, even people who don't drink coffee. There are always a few who do drink coffee but don't join the club. They tend to have their own little pots and drink alone with great apparent gusto. Sometimes they will offer coffee to others, but only in emergencies when the club has failed to provide. Some of these people even bring in thermoses of coffee from home, which betrays a dismaying amount of good organization. However, these coffee drinkers tend to be solitary (perhaps even loners) and do not participate in the camaraderie of the club.

Even worse are the people who stop at the 7-Eleven on their way to work and bring in a large coffee. This allows them to have their coffee and avoid the work. Such people are beneath contempt for the poor program analyst who has just toted a big can of water from the janitor's sink to the coffeemaker. There is nothing more irritating to members of the coffee club than some person sitting at a desk swilling a large commercial coffee.

Most offices now sponsor coffee clubs and many companies (not the government) even pay for the coffee and fixings, maybe even some dry soup and microwave popcorn. This is good business. Not only do the workers like another fringe benefit, but a lot of time is saved because they do not have to leave the office, get on an elevator, go to the first floor, and visit the deli in the next block just to get a cup of coffee. What a waste of time! Even when the company pays for the supplies, however, someone has to do the work, and that means a coffee club.

My advice is for everyone to join the coffee club. The bigger it is, the more it may offer. Now that there are companies to deliver the supplies, the machinery, and even technical advice, making coffee is not as complicated as it used to be. The coffee often comes in premeasured plastic bags, so quality control is no longer a challenge. It really takes effort to mess up the coffee using premeasured bags. If there are enough people, you can even have some goodies like hot water for tea or even some hot soup. But nothing will upset the equilibrium of an office more than a bankrupt coffee club that is merely teetering along and periodically runs out of coffee, never has sugar, and causes fights about who is supposed to make coffee.

Making the coffee is the bottom line. A common rule is that the person who empties the pot makes the next fresh pot. This has amazing effect on drinking habits. Some reluctant coffee drinkers take a half-cup rather than technically empty the pot. Some would rather wait than make. Fortunately, there are always a few in each office who understand the importance of coffee and will leap in and make it. These willing coffee drinkers have the undying gratitude of those who shrink instinctively from work that they apparently feel is demeaning.

It is particularly important to understand clearly who makes the first pot in the morning. There is nothing worse than coming into the office, turning on the lights, looking around at the disarray from the day before, and then going to the coffee mess to find an empty pot or, even worse, the cold, stale remains of yesterday's final pot. Most offices have some lovely person who likes to get in early and make the first pot. This is great! There is nothing better than to walk into the office first thing in the morning to find the lights on and a fresh pot of hot coffee bubbling in the corner. It starts the whole day off right.

Remember, coffee may be the only thing the whole office does together. The coffee club is a reflection of the organization. A good office has a good coffee club, although the reverse is not necessarily true. Better workers should demonstrate their support for their office families by joining the coffee club.

## Rule 47: Avoid Managing the Coffee Club

The wise worker avoids managing the coffee club. There are few positions for which failure is inevitable, but coffee club manager is one. It is a classic lose-lose situation.

The manager's duties appear to be easy. They are to buy the supplies, see that the coffee is made, see that the area is clean, and collect payment for this. These duties are fraught with pitfalls.

Buying supplies is a pain. Clever managers simply hire a coffee service, but these are slightly more expensive and some offices are cheap when it comes to coffee. They may be spending millions of dollars for welfare or defense or modern art in the lobby, but they won't pay more than a nickel for a cup of coffee. In this case the poor coffee manager has to visit the local grocery store on his or her own time, buy the coffee, sweetener, creamer, cups, stirrers, and other stuff, then bring it to the office the next day in a large brown paper bag. This is a real chore, particularly for bus riders. (It is nothing, however, compared with bringing in a birthday cake.) If supplies are handled well, they are only a burden. Most of the time, however, they become an emergency.

It is well known that emergencies arise at the worst possible times. The coffee manager has to prepare a briefing for the vice president, has two other urgent projects, and the typist has phoned in sick. This is when it is discovered that there is no creamer. There suddenly is an urgent need for it. People who don't even like creamer are screaming for it. Time is taken to visit other offices looking for creamer, but foraging is not fruitful in the coffee club business. Few clubs are run well enough to be able to donate supplies, and few managers are generous enough

to do so in any case. The coffee club manager has to drop everything and make an emergency run. This creates great job stress,
but if left undone will result in considerable harassment from
other workers.

Making and cleaning up are also problems. No matter what
the policy about who makes the coffee and who cleans up, it will
not work. The only way is for the coffee club manager to clean
up. Since this is the very reason for being appointed to the job in
most cases, it is what tends to happen. The position of manager
of the coffee club may not be a milepost on the road to the
executive suite, but only another dirty job. As with all dirty jobs,
someone has to do it.

All of the above is a piece of cake compared with the chore
of collecting money. This requires real effort on the part of the
coffee club manager and invokes the greatest protest. Most members will pay promptly when approached, but even the best will
not volunteer to pay without being nagged, or (gasp!) pay in
advance. So even with the good guys, it takes effort to extract
money. With a few employees it is a real pain in the neck. Some
people who drink tea or don't drink much coffee honestly believe that their share is too great, and they appear to resent having
to pay a few bucks for a service that they don't use very much.
Usually, these people will pay up, but only after much nagging.
There are also a few who, one way or the other, refuse to pay,
though they drink the coffee. Sometimes these people simply
"forget" to have money, for days and weeks. Sometimes they just
refuse. Since this is an entirely unofficial deal, the poor coffee
club manager can't court-martial these recalcitrants. So it is a
tough problem. As noted, many clever companies avoid all this by
paying for supplies.

My basic advice is to avoid being coffee club manager. If
taken too much to heart, however, this suggestion would kill that
important institution, so I am tempering my advice by saying that
you should take this job only if you are masochistic or warm-
hearted and understand that managing the club will require great
effort, engender great frustration, and bring little luster to your
career.

# Rule 48: Contribute for Gifts

You will be asked to contribute to mementos for your co-workers. Someone is always collecting for a gift for Nancy, who is retiring; George, who is moving to another office; or Phoebe, who is ill or has had a baby or is getting married or divorced. Always contribute to these collections.

In terms of social organization, you and your co-workers are a small tribe. Your office is a small, relatively simple, self-contained, and homogeneous group associated by your work. As such, your tribe has learned norms that establish rules of behavior and relationships. The tribe shares customs, rituals, and obligations. One of the customs of office worker tribes is to give gifts that observe notable milestones on the highway of life for the members.

If gifts are not given, there is probably something wrong with the office. The giving of gifts is no assurance of a healthy tribe, but the absence of gifts is a sign that the tribe is not working together.

The self-appointed organizer of this gift-giving is always collecting. Sometimes this is the head secretary, sometimes the unofficial office social worker. But there is always someone to take the responsibility. The people who organize the gift purchases and parties are to be congratulated and supported.

You may find that contributing for gifts is not only tiresome but hard on the pocketbook. Nevertheless, to stay in good standing in the tribe, you have to follow the custom. The people who refuse to participate expose themselves as cheapskates and loners. Coughing up two bucks for Muriel's birthday is a small thing, and being unwilling to do that is the act of a small person. If you don't act like a member of your group, you won't be treated as one.

Being a member of the group is important. By adhering to the customs and rituals, you earn respect and support because of the obligation of the group to support you. That is, membership has is duties has well as its benefits.

It is good to give gifts. The act and the thought help to solidify the tribe so that it can work more effectively. The act is important to the person remembered. It is also important to the whole, for it helps make the workplace more friendly and sociable than it would be without these personal touches. So the giving of gifts and flowers needs to be supported informally by management and to be understood as a tribal custom.

Besides, you may have a birthday or retire, and you would like to get a gift yourself. Give generously and you shall receive likewise. But don't look at this in a materialistic manner; the real virtue of giving is to cement your personal commitment to the group.

## Rule 49: Use Lunchtime to Network
You have a half-hour to an hour and a half for lunch each working day. The length of your break depends on your job and the patience of your supervisor.

You can spend your lunch break any way you want. It truly is discretionary time. You can exercise. You can walk around the park. You can visit a museum or go shopping. You can run errands. You can even eat lunch. Eating lunch has a variety of possibilities.

There are four basic styles: brown baggers, lunch bunches, solitaries, and power lunchers.

Brown baggers bring a bag from home, generally brown. They either prepare their own sandwich or salad or, if they are lucky, have a spouse do it for them. Brown baggers do this to save money, save time, avoid lousy food in the cafeteria, or all of the above. Normally, a brown bagger will eat at the desk or in the office lunchroom. Sometimes, however, a group of brown baggers meets as a lunch bunch.

A lunch bunch is a group of workers that meets regularly or intermittently to have lunch. The custom is for a group to go at the same time each day to the local eatery and sit together for lunch. There is usually a hard core that does this every day, and there are some people who join the bunch from time to time. You can see lunch bunches in every cafeteria in the vast complexes of office buildings in cities. Some lunch bunches enjoy a sort of movable feast by going to a different deli or pizza parlor each day. The idea is to swap stories and tell jokes as they eat their tuna sandwiches. This is a friendly and festive occasion that is pleasantly anticipated by the members.

Then there are the solitaries. They can be found at their desk with their brown bag, a sandwich from the deli, or a candy bar from the vending machine, or sitting alone at local eateries. These people sometimes work while eating or eat while working. This is standard for some eager beavers, and all workers do this once in a while during crunches. Some read novels or comic books while munching. Some just stare out of the window. One reason to eat alone is to escape the pressure of communicating. Office work basically produces information, and this involves continuous and seemingly interminable communication. Sometimes people just like to eat lunch alone in order to shut off the noise for a while.

There is the executive solitary luncher. This is the high-ranking person who has his or her secretary get a sandwich or a tray from the cafeteria and deliver it for the official to eat in the office. I think that much of this is just a way to demonstrate that the official is working so hard that time cannot even be taken for a civilized lunch. Some high officials do this all of the time, apparently finding it a hard habit to break. Others just do it enough to impress the lower class. The worst kind of executive solitaries are those who eat their brought-in lunch at their desks while talking business to subordinates who have not yet had lunch. This has happened to me, and it is a true height of insensitivity. Actually, the worst example of this was a 6:00 A.M. meeting with a boss who ate breakfast with relish in front of a room full of hungry workers.

Finally, there are the power lunchers. They go to restaurants rather than eateries. The restaurants range in price from moderate to outrageous, but they all have waiters. Power lunchers seek to share gossip, make deals, and generally advance careers and perhaps goals. These are valuable events and can even be fun. They are generally hard on the diet and the pocketbook. For some bureaucrats, the power lunches become the raison d'être for coming to work. Incidentally, power breakfasts are also "in" to a degree, but only for the highest grades and most ambitious workers who don't mind starting early.

Oh, yes, my advice is to use lunch hours to network. Networking simply means extending your communications with co-workers and colleagues from other offices to increase your knowledge, let others know your estimable qualities, and generally make you a more effective worker. The solitary lunchers trade networking for peace. That is their choice, but it is not necessarily better than using lunch hours to find out what is going on outside your workaday world.

## Rule 50: Listen to Gossip

The more you know, the better you can function. You learn by going to school; by reading newspapers, magazines, books, and memos; by reading the law and regulations; by attending meetings and seminars; and by listening to gossip.

Gossip consists of oral reports about people—who is sleeping with whom, who will get the promotion, who will be promoted to vice president, who said what and when, and similar matters. It can be spicy or dull. It can be nice or nasty. It can be true or false. Gossip is the informal means of spreading rumor, innuendo, insults, opinions, and even facts about other people.

Office gossip generally concerns three kinds of people: co-workers, bosses, and points of contact in other offices involved in the same type of work.

Most shoptalk consists of 80 percent gossip and 20 percent substance.

Gossip has a bad reputation and many people say they will not listen to it. Some who say this actually do not listen. But for most office workers, gossip is a major pastime. What do you think people talk about during coffee breaks, lunch, or bull sessions? Once the football pool has been covered, talk turns to people—gossip.

It will actually be hard to avoid gossip. Every office has one or two individuals who make a career out of it. These people approach you with the tantalizing opening of "Did you hear about George?" It is hard for even the most staid person to resist that kind of opening, so the inevitable result is that you learn all about George. One of my co-workers in the Office of the Secretary of Defense made his rounds each morning for about an hour and then came back to relate to us the most amazing things. His accuracy was high and he learned things that the rest of us could not even imagine. He even predicted correctly who would be appointed secretary of defense during an interregnum. You know the kind of person I mean.

The telephone is a primary means of transmitting gossip. I estimate that one out of four calls made by office workers is devoted to gossip. Two of the remaining three are for personal business and one is for official business.

This is not to say that gossip is useless or counterproductive. Working in a large organization is a very human enterprise; when nothing tangible is being produced, there have to be many human factors involved. And gossip is just a way to satisfy curiosity about the other human beings in your office.

I mentioned earlier that gossip can be bad, neutral, or good. That is a judgment. Predicting the new boss is probably neutral. Relating how the boss messed up a congressional hearing by showing up late and being unable to answer questions is good or bad, depending on one's position. Gossip is a form of knowledge and power. It is sometimes mean and often inaccurate.

The best policy is to listen to gossip that comes your way, take it with a grain of salt, and don't take serious actions based on it. Neither seek nor avoid gossip. It is a fact of office life that may even serve some purpose.

## Rule 51: Don't Spread Gossip

While listening to gossip may be unavoidable and even helpful, you should not spread it. Let the gossip you hear stop with you.

It may be of interest to you that the boss is dating his or her secretary. The knowledge may even be helpful. It is unlikely to bring you credit if you go around repeating it.

Everyone likes gossip, but no one likes gossips. That person in every office who makes a full-time job of talking about other people is seldom respected for good work or a great personality. These people are tolerated but not liked very much. The fellow who spread so much gossip in the Office of the Secretary of Defense was considered a bit weird by the rest of us, even as we listened raptly to his tales.

One reason that gossipers are not really popular is that no one is sure that he or she won't be the victim the next time around. Everyone avoids publicity about some of their actions, and we don't want to be the subject of gossip, false or true. We know that we can be grinning today about poor old George's predicament but that next week we could be the office laughing-stock.

So the best policy is to never spread gossip. Don't say anything malicious or gossipy about other people. If you are going to comment, at least do it consistently within your tight-knit peer group, and then only fairly. If you have a reputation for being closed-mouthed, you will, in fact, become a confidant and the recipient of even more hot tidbits. This may or may not please you. You may even want to avoid gossip, but there is value to knowing not just what is going on but what others say is going on.

No matter what gossip you hear, don't pass it on.

# Rule 52: Never Betray a Confidence

During your career you will receive many confidences. They will be unasked for and unavoidable. The boss may say something about his boss while the two of you are riding to a meeting. A co-worker will sidle up to your desk with the usual words, "Don't tell anyone, but . . ." So you are going to know a lot of secrets about people and events.

You should never betray a confidence. This goes along with Rule 51, but it is even more important. Gossip is general and often unattributable. The source of a confidence is always known.

I really cannot think of any good reason to betray a confidence. The most common motive is to demonstrate just how important and knowledgeable you are by telling a secret. Or, the confidence might be breached in order to do dirt to the person who told you or the subject of the confidence. On rare occasions a betrayal of confidence might be rationalized as an overriding ethical good. Except for the last, the motives are self-serving and insufficient. The best policy is never to betray a confidence.

When you listen to a secret (in the general sense), you enter into a tacit contract. In exchange for learning the secret, you agree to keep it to yourself. If the condition is "don't tell anyone," that is what you must do.

There are practical reasons for this. If you betray a few confidences, you will not get more chances because people will stop confiding in you. Once you are known as a blabbermouth, only fools or masochists will tell you their innermost thoughts or the inside news. If being a confidant is important to you, you must have a reputation for being trustworthy and tight-lipped.

You may not want to hear confidences; if this is so, the way to avoid them is to just say no when one is offered. You then avoid entering into a contract. This will save your reputation and may even enhance it.

If, however, you are entrusted with confidences, simply keep them. Do not succumb to the temptation to show off or take malicious action.

# How to Get Ahead

Getting ahead means being promoted and getting a bigger job with more responsibility, more people to supervise, more power, more perks, and a bigger office. Getting ahead is important to most office workers, yet the competition is tough and not everyone gets ahead. At least not everyone gets ahead as fast or as far as he or she would like. Here are some things you can do to give yourself a competitive advantage.

## Rule 53: Plan Your Career

When you work for a large organization, you have a career, not just a job. A career is a lifetime of work in a field. A career implies progression in pay, prestige, and power along with increases in responsibility. You start at the bottom of the "career ladder" and end up on top twenty-five or thirty years later.

So you have to think about more than just the present job. You have to think about your next job and the one after that. In order to do that, you have to think about your goals. Where do you want to be in twenty-five years?

Most young people (under thirty-five) cannot imagine where they want to be next year, much less than in twenty-five. But it is useful to think about where you want to go so that the steps you take will lead in that general direction.

Time is your most valuable asset and scarcest commodity. You have a fixed amount available. You don't know how much time you have, but most of us simply project ahead to "old age" to imagine things like financial security and retirement. Old age is a variable term, by the way. The years that qualify for old age increase as you get older. Sixty used to be old, but it isn't to most people nowadays. When I was in my teens, I regarded people in their forties as old.

Some people believe that there is a master plan in large organizations to develop careers. They imagine that personnel experts plan the training, assignment, and promotions of the office workers. This is not so. It is certainly not so in the private sector, and despite some smoke and mirrors, it is not so in the government, either. Personnel offices provide opportunity for training, a system for assignments, and assistance in developing careers, but there is no master plan. Your career is up to you.

You should take an active role in determining your jobs, training, and education. No one else is as interested in your career as you are, and no one is going to do you favors. You will have to seize the initiative and take action at the right times to influence where you are going and what you are going to do.

This is risky. You might make a mistake. It happens a lot. People choose the wrong jobs and find themselves dead-ended in their forties. Some people avoid school until it is too late to qualify for higher-graded jobs. Some people are simply misled by bosses who put immediate production ahead of long-range development of more capable employees. Managing your career is not easy, but it is better than just going whichever way fate takes you.

Having said this, there are limits to what you can do for yourself. Most of the time you are stuck in a project team as a junior engineer waiting for some senior engineer to die or retire. Many organizations are like that. The rank, status, and pay of office workers tend to be vested in the job or the position rather than in the individual—at least at the worker level. Because of this, you will have to find a vacant higher-graded position to get a promotion. This means that most organizations have long lists of people waiting to move up when a vacancy occurs. This also means that changing to a job with equal pay—a lateral transfer—is risky because you can end up behind a waiting list you never even knew about. This is why many smart people take lateral transfers only for a promotion, except to get out from under a bad boss.

Schooling is risky, too. Many workers in the private and public sectors believe that some of the most prestigious training and school assignments are given to people not as a reward for hard work or to help them do more important jobs, but to get rid of malcontents and nonproducers. If so, that is a terrible distortion of the schooling function.

There is enough anecdotal evidence to support the conclusion that some misfits *are* sent to school. One federal agency tried to rid itself of a troublemaker by sending him off to school, knowing that he would not get his job back after a year away. Well, it worked just as the agency had planned, except that the troublesome exile did find a new job after his year of school—as staff director of the congressional committee with oversight of the agency. Needless to say, the agency soon regretted having pushed that person outside of the tent.

Many employees also feel that it is dangerous to leave their jobs to go to school because their colleagues will do them in while they are away.

Well, given those beliefs, it is no wonder that many ambitious employees on the fast track avoid schooling like the plague. Despite the prevailing folklore, however, I believe that schooling has become more beneficial to career development in recent years and will become more so in the future.

So my advice is to plan your career and act wisely when opportunity arises. Take advantage of schooling opportunities and shoot for the job you would like next. This does not mean that you should become pushy and flagrantly careeristic. People who think of nothing but the next job most often mess up the present one. These people are so blatant that they injure their careers rather than enhance them.

You should be realistic about your position and potential and be ready to take advantage of opportunities. After all, that is about what most of us can expect out of life.

## Rule 54: Read Up on Your Subject

Knowledge is power. There is so much to know that people who really know their subjects command respect and even awe.

Perhaps you did not have too much choice about your subject area. You may have been recruited for one job and then assigned to another. Your subject may have depended on something as inconsequential as your selection of an empty desk when you reported for work. You may have been working on a contract that ended and then were reassigned to another team entirely. Or, you may have made a choice deliberately. No matter how you did it, there will be a fairly definite subject area that is the focus of your work.

If you are a government employee, chances are that you will remain in your general area for a long time, perhaps even your entire career. Movement in the federal government tends to be vertical along subject lines rather than horizontal from subject to subject. You can start as a budget analyst and remain one for thirty years while working in different offices and even different agencies. In this case your subject matter is the budget, while the numbers change from job to job. You can start as a personnel expert, security specialist, engineer, or communications technician, or any number of areas. You will move about as you move up in grade, but most people will remain in a basic subject area.

If you work in the private sector, you are more likely to shift from subject area to subject area in the course of a career. There seems to be more flexibility than in government. True, even in the private sector, production people stay in production, sales people stay in sales, and financial people stay in finance. It also appears that the opportunity to move laterally starts earlier in a corporation than in the government. However, the likelihood is that you will work in the same general area for a long time in any large organization.

This means that you have a tremendous opportunity to become an expert in that area. It doesn't take too much to become an expert because your fellow workers will be concentrating on their own areas and will know little about yours. You won't be able to fool them, but you can impress them.

One of the best ways to learn about your subject is to read the professional literature on it. In fact, one of the best ways to keep up and get ahead is to read a lot. I assume that as a capable worker, you already read at least one daily newspaper carefully, including the sports section and comics. I also assume that you read a weekly newsmagazine and at least one other general-interest periodical. This lays the foundation for the kind of contemporary knowledge needed by any responsible office worker.

In addition, you should read up on your specific subject matter. As a minimum, I recommend the following:

1. Read the laws, regulations, reports, and other official documentation on your subject area. This is very important. Such material is available and may be read on government time, yet too few people avail themselves of this method (see Rule 25).

2. Read at least one professional journal for your subject area.

3. Obtain a list of the ten most important books in your subject area and read them systematically. Get the list from some co-worker or boss in your subject area whom you respect as an expert.

4. Try to read two or three new books a year in your subject area.

The mark of a professional is knowledge of his or her subject. Reading up on the subject matter is the first step toward becoming a true professional.

# Rule 55: Take Any Short Course You Can

There are lots of short classes or training courses for office workers. Corporations and government agencies sponsor many courses in an effort to improve the quality and knowledge of the work force. Many last only a few days or one or two weeks.

My advice is to attend as many of these short courses as you can. You will gain a lot of knowledge that will be useful in the long run. Some of the offerings will clearly be in your subject area and will improve your expertise on the job. Others will be remote from your current duties but will broaden your perspective. Either way, you will improve your value to your organization and your boss.

Many people avoid short courses because they feel they have too much work to do or because they are afraid to be away from their desks. Some bosses oppose short courses because they feel they have too much work to do or because they are afraid to allow their people to be away from their desks. These reasons are understandable but shortsighted.

The work will always be there. I have never known there to be a shortage of work. If a worker leaves for a week, there is likely to be little change in the immediate work load. So not going to short courses because of work load is correct but not relevant to long-term improvement of the work force. Opposing short courses because of fear of having people absent is based on severe job insecurity and cannot be cured by reason.

Some bosses look on short courses as thinly disguised vacations. They believe that going to school is fun. Well, it is fun, but it also can help the boss's organization—at least in the long run. There is no reason to oppose something of value just because it also is pleasant.

Basically, however, it is up to the employee to judge the risk of being away from the desk versus the value of learning something. This will vary for each job, boss, and course. Generally, it is good to go to as many short courses as you can.

# Rule 56: Attend Seminars and Conferences

Another way to improve your expertise is to attend seminars and conferences.

You will have lots of chances to attend communication events in your subject area. If you have taken my advice to read a professional journal, you will probably have joined a professional society. The society sponsors meetings and special events for members.

There also is an entire industry that conducts meetings. There are seminars, conferences, and shows of all sizes, types, and subjects.

You should try to attend at least some of these. As with attendance at short courses, there are pros and cons. It would be wrong to spend all of your time at these events; it would be equally wrong to avoid all of them.

These meetings are communications events. Their purpose is to disseminate information on a particular subject. Some information is fundamental and aimed at new people. Much is new stuff designed to keep old practitioners up on new developments. All are designed to improve your knowledge of your area.

My experience is that no matter how knowledgeable you are, you will learn something from these meetings. A new idea, a new relationship between old ideas, or a new way of looking at things is of great value.

These meetings facilitate extraordinary communications. During your official work you are restricted on whom you can talk to, what you can say, and just sheer time limitations. Normally, you have to parrot official or corporate positions, guard your tongue, and prepare memos for the record. Normally, you wouldn't think of talking to some peasant from the field organization of another agency. Normally, you wouldn't swap stories with a competitor. Normally, you wouldn't have the chance to talk to an assistant secretary of another agency. So the opportunity you have to communicate during official work hours is limited in many ways. At these seminars and meetings, however, you can communicate more freely.

In fact, these communications events are structured largely to circumvent constraints on your communications during work hours. People of different ranks gather in an informal structure that promotes open discussion. You can talk substance or process rather than personalities or politics. You can chat with an assistant secretary or a worker from another corporation. You can find out from the field worker just what the real world is like. You can open your mind to different views, and even different facts, without feeling threatened. There is much to be gained by attending communication events.

## Rule 57: Speak on Your Subject

Another way to improve yourself and your reputation is to speak on your subject at seminars, conventions, and meetings.

You will learn a lot by preparing to speak. Writing speeches or papers for presentation is the true test of subject mastery. There is a great deal of difference between being a student and a teacher; the student is essentially a passive receptor. The teacher is an emitter of knowledge. It takes a lot more time, care, and sheer intellectual effort to emit than to receive. So the very act of preparing your presentation will force you to learn about your subject.

The presentation itself will improve you also. Exposure of your ideas and logic to the slings and arrows of outraged fellow experts can be exhilarating, humbling, exasperating, and all of the above. You will be forced to defend concepts you believed to be self-evident. You will have to crystallize half-formed ideas. You will be challenged, disputed, and denied. All of this, of course, is healthy even though uncomfortable. You will learn more, assuming you do not get defensive and close your mind under intellectual attack.

Of course, speaking before groups with similar interests leads to a sympathetic rather than hostile audience. You will not have to put up with a lot of flak from most groups. Many in the group will have gone through the same experience and will go easy on you the first few times. Once you have demonstrated some capability, you can expect and will deserve more rigorous treatment.

Finally, and perhaps most important, speaking to groups will hone your presentation skills. Speaking before groups is a big emotional barrier to many people, but it is an essential skill in business and government. Any midlevel worker who cannot address a group with ease is limiting his or her advancement. The

best way to learn to speak before groups is to do it, so seek out
the chance to make presentations before like-minded groups.

## Rule 58: Write Articles on Your Subject

If you want to become known as a real expert, write articles.
Research and writing also increase proficiency in your subject,
for you will have to put down your thoughts coherently. Another
benefit is that you will spread your ideas in your community and
perhaps influence policy.

There are a lot of possibilities. Every subject has publications
dealing exclusively with it, and there are general magazines that
may accept articles on your subject. There are newsletters published by all kinds of clubs and associations. In fact, there is an
amazing number of periodicals in the United States and each
needs material.

One place to start is with the professional or trade associations dealing with your subject. Almost all professional associations publish a journal. Articles for these publications tend to
be scholarly and are reviewed before being accepted. Trade and
special-interest associations publish articles of interest to their
members. Smaller special-interest groups need copy for their
newsletters.

If you are serious about writing, you may wish to consult
editors on subjects of interest to them. You may prefer to write
about something dear to your heart. Unless you intend to be a
professional writer rather than a better worker, stick to things that
you know.

The next step is to write the article. This is not as easy to do
as it is to say. The only way to do it is to sit down and hammer it
out. This requires a particular staying power, "sitzfleisch," which
implies that you will stay at it until the article is written. This is
not a book on writing, so I will leave it at that.

It is important to have the proper equipment. Using a pencil
and legal pad is terribly old-fashioned and inefficient. A typewriter is almost as bad. The tremendous power of word processing makes the sheer job of writing much less onerous than before.
That is one reason for the explosion in publications. If you can

afford the best, get a laser printer. This will make it a lot easier than you ever thought possible to produce good-looking articles. Having good equipment allows you to concentrate on the content rather than the tedious job of putting it on paper.

Unfortunately, there is a lot more to this than just writing the article. The hard part is getting it published. Though there are hundreds of periodicals to be filled up each month, there are thousands of writers submitting articles. It is particularly difficult for first-time authors to break in.

The only way to do it is to write an article and submit it. Only big names get contracts for articles on the basis of outlines or concepts. You will have to write the whole thing and send it in. Allow lots of lead time. Most monthly magazines work four to six months ahead. And don't count on getting rich from this. Periodicals do not pay big bucks for articles written by government or business workers. Moreover, regular government employees may be forbidden to accept payment for articles. Since the whole idea is to make a name for yourself and/or contribute to your subject area, don't worry about the money. If you do the work on corporation or government time as part of your official duties and with permission of your supervisor, you will at least get paid while doing the writing.

My advice is to give these ideas serious consideration. Writing for publication is not everyone's cup of tea, and if you hate to write papers or memos, don't try articles. But if you worked on the school newspaper and thought you might like to write someday, this is the time to start.

# Rule 59: Join an Interest Group

Another way to learn more about your subject area and to be perceived as an expert is to join an interest group.

Chances are there is an interest group for your field, no matter how esoteric the subject is. There are interest groups on every subject from analysis to zoology. If there is more than one person doing something, there is an interest group.

Ask around for the group in which you are interested. Some are large, formal organizations that deal with a broad field in business or government. Some are professional associations for comptrollers or operations research analysts. Some are associated by status or schooling, such as a chamber of commerce, the Senior Excecutives Association, or the Federal Executive Institute Alumni Association. Some are smaller, informal, and relatively unorganized. These might include a computer user group, a club devoted to farm cooperatives, or a loose group that meets periodically to discuss common concerns. There are many sizes and flavors and you have to pick one that suits your personality and needs.

The important thing is to be involved and to extend your grasp beyond the mere job. You will find that almost all large organizations encourage a reasonable degree of participation in these groups, recognizing the value in learning, in spreading the official line, and in marketing. So you will find that you can do a lot of these things on working time.

There are limits to this, so don't get ridiculous. Make certain that the activities you want underwritten by your employer are job-related.

There are some pitfalls with these associations. All groups have a purpose. Sometimes it is pure information exchange, along with some fun. Sometimes the associations lobby hard for positions favored by their members. In this case you may find yourself in a bind because your organization does not want what the association wants. By joining a lobbying organization, of course, you are asking to be lobbied. Just know of this danger as you participate. Remember, some people are trying to co-opt you.

You may wish to help manage an organization. This is hard work and usually is voluntary, without even reimbursement for expenses. You may find it rewarding. Certainly the success of most interest groups depends on a few hard-working volunteers. These people always get the job done. If you decide to participate actively, be ready for the increased workload. Your extracurricular activities may hurt your job performance, so you will have to make an arrangement with your boss or cut back on outside stuff. The job comes first, no matter how rewarding or enhancing the interest group is.

# Supervising

When you do get ahead by following the last set of rules, one of your rewards is likely to be that you will become a supervisor. A supervisor has one or more other employees working for him or her. The very name implies your biggest responsibility: supervising others in their work. In short, you will become a boss.

Being a boss carries with it tremendous responsibility as well as more money, prestige, perks, and power. There is an ongoing argument in psychological circles about whether good supervisors are made or born. Without taking sides in this burning controversy, we can all agree that a few simple rules can help you become a better supervisor. These are extensions of the basic rule, which is the office version of the Golden Rule: Be the kind of boss you would like to have for your boss.

## Rule 60: Treat Your People Well
This should go without saying. The first rule of management is to treat your people well. This is taught in all Management 101 courses.

Unfortunately, it is often ignored. I am amazed by the number of supervisors who think that the way to get their employees to work hard is to act like dictators. Too many bosses treat their people like dirt. They yell at them, put them down in front of others, ridicule them, and ignore their needs. These same bosses expect these people to work extra hard to get a tough job done well and on time!

If you are lucky enough to be a supervisor and have people helping you do your work, you should treat them just the way you wanted to be treated when you were starting out. I do not mean the way your supervisor treated you, but how you would have liked. Unless you are a first-class masochist, you wanted to be treated nicely. Do the same for your own staff.

It takes less energy to be nice than to be mean. You can smile, say hello, use the "P" word, and exercise common courtesy in dealing with subordinates. It will not lessen your authority; in fact, it will make you a more effective leader than if you act mean.

I learned in Management 101 about McGregor's idea on management style. A Theory X manager approaches people as if they did not want to work and had to be driven to it. A Theory Y manager assumes that people want to work and only need an environment in which to do it. I believe in Theory Y. Almost all employees want to work and, given the chance, will do a good job. Good supervisors will foster this by encouraging their workers.

The biggest complaint I find among workers is that they seldom are allowed to do their best because of officious, overbearing, and frightened bosses who insist on rewriting all documents and oversupervising their staff but still cannot make decisions. These same supervisors, of course, can be counted on to treat their people poorly and then justify it by their own lack of output. Few people are honest enough to acknowledge that they are at fault, and this is particularly true for managers who don't have enough sense to treat their people well.

If you read this, you at least are interested enough to introspect. You probably care about your work. You will advance it if you also care—really care—about and for your workers, too.

# Rule 61: Give Credit to Your People

There are two kinds of people in an organization: those who write papers they do not sign and those who sign papers they do not write. You figure out which group contains the bosses.

One consequence is that the people who sign the papers tend to get the credit for them. An article appears in the editorial section of the *Washington Post* signed by the assistant secretary of something, and the public assumes that the assistant secretary wrote the thing. Not so. The article was written by a junior program analyst and reviewed by a senior program analyst, a branch chief, a division chief, and five senior executives before it got to the assistant secretary. There were revisions along the way, but the essence remained intact as "woulds" were changed to "shoulds" and back again. So the assistant secretary gets the credit. That is the way it has to be. It is a simple fact of life that no one would pay attention to an article signed by Martha Greene, junior program analyst.

The same thing is true in the private sector. The annual report of the president was probably written by an assistant several layers lower, vetted up the line, and finally revised a bit and signed by the Big Boss. This is not wrong. Big bosses must think a lot, and while writing reports is important, the bosses should utilize their staffs to do a lot of the work. So the bosses should get all the help they can, and acknowledge that help.

Within a hierarchy, let credit fall where it belongs. Good managers have always known this. A good assistant secretary takes the time to write a note to Ms. Greene, junior program analyst, commending her for the excellent article. A good corporate president will let the drafters of his annual report know that their good job was appreciated. This costs little but has a big payoff in morale and team cohesion. Every junior program analyst and staff assistant will knock his or her socks off trying to do a great job on the next article, project, paper, or report.

Unfortunately, not all bosses are that enlightened. Some do not give credit to those who did the work. Some bosses pretend that they did the work themselves. Some bosses start believing that they did. This leads to poor morale, team dissension, and less effort by the worker bees.

So if you are a boss, my advice is to give the credit for good work to the person who did the work. You have everything to gain and nothing to lose. You can bask in the reflected glory of your staff's accomplishment and take credit for being smart enough and good enough to have such an outstanding crew.

At the next staff meeting when the executive vice president looks at you and says, "The report on the McGregor matter was very good," you can say something like, "Thank you. Martha Greene worked very hard on that and really pulled it together." You can then tell Martha that a Big Boss complimented her work. Everyone wins!

## Rule 62: Take the Blame Yourself

This rule has to do with responsibility and authority. You may delegate authority, but you may never delegate responsibility. You are responsible for everything that goes on in your organization. If good things happen, you get the credit. If bad things happen, you get the blame. This is a primary principle of organization.

You cannot have it both ways. If you intend to get promotions, bonuses, attention, and power because of the work done by your staff, then you have to take the blame for the errors, too.

It used to be in the U.S. Navy that a captain of a ship had absolute responsibility for it. If the ship ran aground or collided with another ship, the captain was relieved of command and court-martialed. It was his fault. It did not matter if the real culprit was a junior officer or petty officer or seaman; the captain was responsible and took the blame. This was not fair, nor was it intended to be fair. It was intended to promote in captains a high degree of interest in making no mistakes at all. It was a powerful incentive to running a tight ship (which we all admire in principle but avoid serving on in practice).

Unfortunately, this principle of responsibility has been weakened in recent years. Even in the Navy, captains have been allowed to blame subordinates for errors and get away with it. Nevertheless, the boss still has to stand for something.

So my advice is to work a reasonable compromise between the stern old Navy standard and the other extreme, which is to pass all blame immediately and directly to a subordinate. Neither situation is workable in civilian life. The best course of action is for you to take on your shoulders the responsibility for the actions of your team, branch, division, or directorate. You should accept the blame for everything that goes wrong. If your boss points up an error, don't say something like, "Jones messed that up. I told him how to do it, but he ignored me." This tells your boss some things about you—that you can't get Jones to follow your orders and you cannot be relied upon because you avoid responsibility. In this situation just say, "Yes, we made an error. I will fix it." Then get hold of Jones and make the correction to him or her directly and privately.

This is not an easy rule to follow. It is hard to take the blame when some idiot working for you was the one who actually messed up. That is one of the reasons you get more pay and prestige than your subordinates. The extra pay is for taking the blame, even when you are blameless.

# Rule 63: Support Your People in Public

No one is perfect. You will make mistakes. Your people will make mistakes. Sometimes an employee needs to be called to account and corrected for mistakes. The way in which corrections are given is important.

You probably have seen a public chewing-out administered by some irate boss to a crestfallen employee. If you are a normal human being, you were very uncomfortable at watching public humiliation. If you were uncomfortable being a witness to the spectacle, imagine how the victim felt.

Some bosses seem to delight in showing their power in public. They give orders loudly and arrogantly, boast about achievements real and imaginary, and humiliate subordinates. The worst expression of arrogance and bad leadership is public humiliation.

Nothing good comes from a public humiliation. The person being humiliated is angry. Though survival and good politics may require outward calm, the victims seethe inside. Their natural reaction is to resent and dislike the tormentor. If the object is to correct a mistake, the words are best said in private, and the tone should be helpful rather than hurtful. If the object is to assert authority, the best way is to be soft-spoken and calm. Real authority does not need to be expressed as arrogant and insensitive treatment of people who cannot fight back.

My advice is to resist any temptation to chew your people out in public. You can express displeasure, but do it in a way that is acceptable to the workers and does not create discomfort in bystanders. There is room in the lexicon of leadership for spot correction. This should be done when an error is detected, and immediate action is indicated. But moderation is good even in spot corrections. To carry on beyond the acceptable tone and length of a correction is humiliating.

Above all, never get personal when making corrections. Remember that the object is to enforce the rules, not belittle the employee. Concentrate on the offending action, not the offender. Do not call the employee stupid, idiotic, or treacherous. If you want to lecture, nag, or carry on beyond more than a simple spot correction, have the offender come into your office for a private chat.

You will also have to support your people if they are attacked in public for their mistakes. You will have to support them in public even if they are wrong, or you will lose a good worker and the respect of your team. You cannot allow anyone to bully your troops. You cannot help someone else gang up on an employee.

Suppose that your boss, the project manager, has just discovered a mistake by one of your employees and chews the person out in front of you and the other workers on your team. The boss castigates the hapless worker and informs him or her of deficiencies in capability and character and really humiliates the poor person. Or suppose a boss from a neighboring division finds a mistake by one of your workers and attacks him or her for inefficiency, treason, or worse, right in front of you and your other workers. You cannot just stand there and allow one of your people to be chewed out by this other boss, no matter how high ranking the other boss is.

In this situation you should support your worker in public. Admit nothing; say nothing to the worker. Close off the discussion as quickly and harmlessly as possible. Get the other people back to work. Then take the offender into your office and discuss the mistake calmly. If you believe it necessary, take the complainant into your office also, but I don't recommend it if you can avoid it.

You are responsible for all of the work done in your branch, team, division, or whatever. If an employee of yours makes a mistake, it is the same as if you made it, so you cannot allow your people to take abuse from anyone but you.

It is your job as boss to take the abuse or the blame. It also is your job as boss to deflect this kind of treatment from your staff, even when it's wrong—particularly when it's wrong. As well, you must make appropriate corrections so that the mistake will not be made again.

You may have to go so far as to banish a poaching boss who is chewing out one of your workers. If the irate boss is your boss, it is touchy, but you still have to be firm.

Get the situation under control. Let things cool off, then investigate. Above all, do it in private so that the poor worker who made the mistake and is already upset about that does not have to suffer additional humiliation by being disciplined in front of his or her peers.

Best results are achieved by treating people as human beings rather than as peons. Your workers will meet your expectations generally. If you treat them poorly, humiliate them in public, or allow them to be humiliated in public, you can expect them to work poorly and give you your just desserts. Remember the office motto: "Never get mad, just get even."

# Rule 64: Respect Your Employees

One of the most amazing things I have noted is the unwillingness of many bosses to respect their subordinates. Often, they won't take their advice or even listen to their ideas and suggestions. Often, bosses reward success by poor treatment and neglect to keep their employees informed. This is just plain crazy.

The whole purpose of an organization is to transcend the limits of what a single person can do by building a social structure that acts together to accomplish massive, complex tasks. One person—no matter how strong or smart—could not have built the pyramids; it took an organization.

An organization depends on the flow of information—down, up, and sideways. Missions, guidance, and the situation flow down from the top. Products, problems, and ideas flow up from the bottom. Proposed actions and requests for support flow sideways in the coordination process. The whole system of information feedback is designed to allow the organization to direct its individual members toward a common goal. This cannot work unless there is mutual respect—down, up, and sideways.

Unfortunately, mutual respect is not always there. Bosses commonly show disrespect for the workers by their actions and pronouncements. Of course, this provokes a lack of respect by the workers for their bosses. Organizations that lack mutual respect internally are not often held in high respect by other organizations. Giving and earning respect has to start at the top—with the boss.

I know some bosses who really shot themselves in the foot by incredibly stupid treatment of their best worker. The employee was a salesperson who was selling more than anyone else, and in fact more than the rest of the sales force combined. The company had been languishing until this employee came on board and boosted sales even higher than the bosses had imagined possible. Instead of rewarding this person and encouraging others to emulate the ace, the bosses reduced her commissions on the ground that her pay was too high at the original rate. They restricted her sales by requiring a detailed telephone log and formal reports. When the sales manager position became open, they selected an outsider who knew nothing about sales and immediately started harassing the worker with the best record. The employee then took her skills elsewhere. Most of the other sales people left shortly thereafter and the sales of the organization decreased dramatically. This was a classic case of managerial incompetence.

Why did they do that? I believe jealousy was the major factor. The bosses simply could not stand to see this lower-ranking person make more money on commissions than they were making in salary, though it helped the organization.

In another instance a first-line supervisor repeatedly scorned productivity improvements suggested by some of his workers. The supervisor never listened. He never understood that improvements in output would make him look good. He simply was not a big enough person to take advice from a subordinate. The employees, frustrated at being treated like mushrooms, quit to seek jobs where they would get some respect and at least be heard.

It is also amazing how many bosses neglect the simple but true maxim of keeping the troops informed. I have been around many organizations, and ignorance seems endemic. Most workers are simply not being kept informed by their bosses. This is so despite great efforts to keep people informed with memos, newsletters, and magazines. This creates great uncertainty, anxiety, and stress. Rumors are rampant in any organization that lacks current, authoritative information from the top. Time spent listening to rumors and speculating does not contribute to getting the job done. This is all obvious and has been pointed out in numerous management classes, but it still seems that workers in most organizations find out what is happening through the grapevine.

My rule is simple. Respect your employees. Reward and encourage good performance. Listen to them. Treat their suggestions and complaints seriously. Keep them informed. They will respect you for it.

# Rule 65: Remember Your Secretary during Secretaries Week

If you are fortunate enough to rate a secretary, you should always remember him or her during Secretaries Week.

A secretary can be a most valuable helper to the manager or executive. A secretary can maximize productivity and minimize aggravation. A secretary can type letters, process documents, maintain the calendar, set up appointments, handle travel arrangements, answer routine inquiries, and provide real support in a crunch. A secretary can be a strong right arm.

Unfortunately, this does not often happen in large organizations—private or public. Many secretaries are improperly used or underused. There tend to be too many secretaries at the top, too few in the middle, and none at the bottom. The vice presidents and the assistant secretaries have fleets of secretaries. Sometimes even their secretaries have secretaries. This is more an ego trip than good work organization. The secretaries are perks, designed to make the big boss look important. It works. The midlevel managers, however, generally have a single secretary who must serve not only the boss but the entire branch, division, or team. The professional workers—engineers, analysts, and programmers—have no secretary except for the one who is supposed to help the boss.

This distribution means that it is either feast or famine for secretarial productivity. They are either typing continuously or reading the newspaper. Those at the top have too little to do and those at the bottom have too much.

The situation is particularly bad in the government. The people in the federal government who work on staff organization apparently believe that it is improper and even immoral to provide enough secretaries to handle all of the work. It is common to find one secretary trying to serve four or five professionals as well as a branch chief. This means that the secretary can do only one thing—type—all day and often all evening. There is just too much typing to be done, so the secretary can't provide other services to workers. This means that highly paid professionals must answer telephones, copy documents, and perform other administrative support chores while the overburdened secretary is chained to the word processor. This is inefficient and invulnerable to reason. The ratio of clerical to professional employees is established in the government according to perceptions of luxury rather than work load.

This situation has eased somewhat lately, for two reasons. Many professionals have their own personal computers and printers. With a good computer, some good software, and a high-quality printer (especially a laser printer), the professional can turn out good-looking documents without a secretary. Also, new approaches to manpower controls in the government and in some private companies allow managers some flexibility in spending their personnel budgets. This could allow managers to increase team output by having two secretaries instead of one midlevel professional for the same amount of salary.

Many executives simply do not know how to use a secretary effectively. Few think about how they should work with their secretaries as a team. Some simply ignore the secretary in the vain hope that he or she will know what to do automatically. Some tend to oversupervise, telling the secretary in detail what and how to do everything. This is understandable, for there are few management classes on how to use a secretary properly.

The secret to making the best use of a secretary is communicating and planning. It is necessary to think about what the role and mission of the secretary are to be, not just hope that he or she can gain this by osmosis. You should tell your secretary what you want, and do it as often as necessary. A short planning meeting each morning will establish the agenda for both people. I have noticed that some of the best executives treat their secretaries with respect and consideration; that undoubtedly makes for a good team as well.

This rule is also a reminder that your secretary is valuable in your business life and that you should show how much you appreciate him or her. This can be done anytime, but it is especially nice to do it each year during National Secretaries Week in April. Give some flowers and a card, then take your secretary to lunch at a nice place during the week. It is the least you can do.

# Rule 66: Deliver the News Yourself, Good or Bad

One of your responsibilities as a supervisor is to deliver the news to the people who work for you. You get to deliver the good news, and you are obligated to deliver the bad news too.

Delivering good news is easy. It is fun to announce promotions and give out medals and certificates. Few supervisors shy away from delivering the good news. They arrange elaborate ceremonies, invite the families, and make a big deal out of good news. A photographer is always present and pictures of the boss handing out the goodies are displayed prominently on bulletin boards and in organizational newsletters and magazines. Giving out good news is a duty every boss relishes.

It is not so with the bad news. For some reason, a lot of bosses do not tell employees about demotions, reassignments, separations for cause, or failures to be selected for jobs. We all have heard about the high-level appointees who first found out about being fired by reading it in the newspaper. That form of notification is at least dignified. Most lower-level employees get the bad news when the moving team shows up.

I know of an incident in which two midlevel employees were competing for the same division chief job. One of the employees, George, was acting division chief and had the big office. The other candidate, Jim, worked in the same division for George. The boss selected Jim for the job, which was his prerogative, but the first that George heard that he had not been selected was when the movers showed up. George was moved peremptorily out of the big office with windows into a smaller, interior office. Jim was moved into the big office. George had to deal not only with his failure to be selected and the prospect of working for his former subordinate but also with the humiliation caused by the way this situation was handled. It was difficult, but to his credit he stuck it out as a loyal and valuable employee.

The general leadership rule is that the one who makes the decision has to announce it. If you create the bad news for some employee, you should make the announcement. You should call that person into your office and tell him or her the news. This will not ease the shock or pain, but it will allow that individual to retain some dignity.

The organization also benefits from this practice. If the employee has potential but simply lost out to a better candidate, as was the case above, a chat could result in the employee trying even harder. If the employee has an attitude that resulted in the bad news, a chat could improve the attitude. If the employee is hopeless, a chat would do nothing at all, but it still should be done.

If you are embarrassed by this kind of thing or haven't the heart to deliver bad news, then you have no business being a boss.

## Rule 67: Bring Home a Victory Now and Then

This bit of advice is for bosses. It is for big bosses and little bosses, from team chiefs to chief executive officers: Bring home a victory now and then.

One of the roles of a boss is that of tribal chief. Organizations are like tribes in that they have distinct cultures—shared values and modes of behavior. All the things discussed in this book— parties, celebrations, even work habits—are tribal rituals. The purpose of these rituals is to appease the unknown gods who work mysteriously to affect the tribe and promote tribal solidarity. There is no better way to promote tribal solidarity than to win a victory in the perpetual office wars.

An office is in constant strife. The fighting is over power, prestige, authority, money, promotions, and sometimes even issues and principles. The more mundane motives for combat go under the collective name of "turf." The primary motive for turf fights is to be in charge of a particular area of office endeavor. Then there are the truly great battles over what is to be done. These substantive battles can be even more serious and be taken more seriously than turf fights, so the system is in a state of perpetual war.

There is not much that can be done about this. It appears to be the human condition. At least in office wars, the cost is bankruptcy, broken careers, and shattered dreams rather than defeat, broken bones, and shattered bodies. Most of the fighting is rather benign and harmless, except to egos.

The wise tribal chief takes care to win some of these skirmishes. If the boss is a constant loser in the wars, the troops will lose confidence and seek a stronger boss. If the boss wins all of the time, the flak from other tribes (the losers) will make it uncomfortable for the winners. Also, shifting alliances will bring against the winner a coalition powerful enough to assure eventual defeat. So win some of the time, lose gracefully some of the time, and make peace most of the time.

Even so, in order to stimulate the tribe and literally give it something to cheer about, the wise chief goes out and wins one now and then.

# Office Ethics

The very phrase "office ethics" is thought to be an oxymoron. Nothing could be farther from the truth. Pound for pound, government employees and those of corporations and other large organizations are as honest as any other group of well-paid, middle-class Americans. As a group they also tend to be ethics conscious and ethical in their behavior.

This good behavior is even more remarkable when one reflects that the environment in government and commerce fails to provide positive incentives to reinforce ethical behavior. The basic assumption of those who set up the rules for the government is that all employees are dishonest. The basic assumption of commerce regulators is that businesspeople are dishonest. Thus, there is heavy emphasis on detailed rules and regulations, complicated processes with numerous approvals, and signatures galore. Workers are always expected to certify this or that, usually under penalty of imprisonment or fine or both. There is a fetish about separating authority from responsibility. The idea is that if those who have to do the work have the required authority, they would probably do something dishonest. The upshot is that the laws, rules, and regulations make it very difficult for honest people to get anything done at all, while the crooks flourish. People who do not hesitate to lie, cheat, or steal have no difficulty defeating any system. The more complicated the system, the easier it is for crooks to defeat.

There are crooks in all organizations. Justice is supposed to punish just the evildoers, but in commerce and government, that is rare. When a crook is caught, the innocent are always punished along with the guilty. Congress reacts with a new law "tightening up" sloppy management. The crooks make a deal, plead extenuating circumstances, and go free. The rest of the employees are imprisoned in the new rules. After a few of these cases, it is a wonder that employees retain their personal codes of ethics, to say nothing of their ideals. Nevertheless, it is always good to reinforce ethical behavior. The next set of rules is intended to do just that.

## Rule 68: Speak the Truth

This is a tough rule. Speaking the truth can be inconvenient and hard. It is likely to get you in trouble and may not even earn you respect. The only reward will be self-respect, whatever that is worth.

Speaking the truth has virtue only when the consequences are adverse. There is no merit in speaking the truth when it is either helpful or neutral. That is, when someone asks the time, there is no particular virtue in giving the correct answer, which is neutral. When the boss asks, "Who wrote this great speech?" there is no problem with acknowledging that you did.

The real test comes when the boss asks, "Who wrote this lousy speech?" So there is virtue in telling the truth only when the truth hurts.

There is also no real virtue in telling the truth when the answer can be determined by other means. When the boss asks who wrote the lousy speech, he probably knows you did and just wants a public confession for the good of your soul. Lying about a fact at a staff meeting would be stupid as well as dishonest.

No, the real test of telling the truth is when only you know it and it will be bad for you. When the boss asks who left the lights on last night and you admit it, even though there was no way to find out about it, there is some virtue for confessing to such a trivial violation. When the boss asks who left the safe open last night and again there is no way to identify the culprit, telling the truth has real virtue because the penalty for a security violation is severe.

Telling the truth is necessary for real communication in any organization. If you are surrounded by habitual liars, it is difficult to tell what is real and what is not. This, you may recall, was Alice's situation in Wonderland. Much time and effort goes into separating truth from fiction. It is simply more efficient and better all around to be able to rely on the statements of others.

Honesty is still the best policy, particularly when it really hurts.

# Rule 69: Give a Day's Work for a Day's Pay

You are paid well by your employer for what you do. This is true whether you work for the government or a company. You probably don't believe you are being paid well enough. That is natural. Few of us believe we are paid what we are really worth. Most of us believe other people are paid more than they are worth.

There is a lot of controversy about pay comparability between the government and the private sector. Almost all government employees believe that they are underpaid compared with those lucky people out there in the private sector who are getting rich. Private-sector employees know that some of them can earn more than the congressional pay ceilings allow their government counterparts to earn. Private-sector employees also know that most of them don't earn the big bucks, and, more important, they can get fired in a minute. Well, I have worked on both sides of that fence, and I am not going to get into a fight over who gets paid better. I will just leave it that organization workers as a whole are paid well.

All office workers fill out time cards purporting to reflect their work hours per pay period. The pay period is either a month or, more commonly nowadays, two weeks. The government and private sector treat time cards differently. In the government, the presumption is that each employee works eighty hours per two-week pay period unless there is annual leave, sick leave, or other exceptions noted on the card. For full-time government employees, the time card is really a record of leave, not of hours worked. In the private sector the time card is really a record of time worked. Even employees who, like most government employees, get an annual salary have to report their time and the projects upon which they worked.

Most office workers are essentially free to spend their workdays as they see fit. This is particularly true of midlevel professionals. While there are office hours and specified lunch breaks, these are not enforced rigidly in most offices. Some bosses make a big deal out of getting to work on time, and some monitor closing time and lunch hours. A few bosses even require their people to take an hour's annual leave to visit the doctor. Most of the time, however, office workers can have a coffee break, get a haircut, see the doctor, exercise, visit a friend, or even shop without taking annual leave or losing an hour of work on the time card.

There is nothing wrong with this. Large organizations expect their highly paid workers who deal with important issues to be mature enough to give a day's work for a day's pay. How can you trust a manager to run a $20 million project and then carp about twenty extra minutes for lunch on Tuesday? How can you expect a trusted secretary to take leave each time he or she buys a gift at the mall? How can you expect a sales representative who has to ask permission to go to the bathroom to ooze enthusiasm to customers? How can you treat people like children and expect them to behave as responsible adults?

For most people this is not a problem. Most put in more than their required eight hours each day. They come in early and stay late. Some work weekends to keep up. Even those entitled to overtime pay often do not record it. So most people do make up for that long lunch hour or haircut or errand by working extra minutes or even hours.

A few people dog it. They put in the hours and get paid, but they do little work. They read magazines and the newspaper, drink coffee, wander around the halls, visit the shopping mall, take long lunches, and even conduct personal business on company or government time. Some employees operate sideline businesses during work hours. These people are freeloaders and thieves because they are paid for hours they didn't work.

My advice is to make certain that your employer gets eight good hours of work from you each workday. One of the advantages of being an office worker is that most of the time you will be allowed to manage your own time. Don't take undue advantage of this privilege.

# Rule 70: Start Something—Anything!

Once in a while the cogs of an organization slip a little and you find yourself with nothing to do. The boss has not given you an impossible deadline; the system has not rejected your last paper. You actually are ahead of the game. Time hangs heavy on your hands.

What you do in this circumstance is the true mark of your character. It is all too easy to do nothing. You can just remain behind your desk, impervious to the rest of the world, and vegetate until a tasking comes down from above. You can take long lunches. You can work crossword puzzles or read the paper. There are all sorts of things you can do to waste time when you don't have to do anything.

However, it is at this crucial time that you can also exercise that highly prized trait of "initiative." You can start something.

You can use the free time to get some work done. Surely there are things that you have put off consciously or unconsciously until you had the time. Now is the time. Do the filing that you have deferred. Write that memo that you postponed. Clean out your hold drawer. Answer some correspondence that has gathered dust for weeks. Return your phone calls. Make some calls of your own. Just don't sit around waiting to be told what to do.

Time is your most precious resource. Like all resources, it is limited. There are only twenty-five hours in the office worker's day, so you have to use time wisely. After deducting sleep, eating, commuting, saying hello to the spouse and kids, participating in community activities, and taking coffee breaks, there is little enough for real work. You should seize the moment.

My advice is to start something during those periodic lulls. Either catch up on your own work or, if you are particularly daring or ambitious, initiate some new work. Show your energy and drive. It will make you unpopular with your less-aggressive co-workers, but it might earn you a reputation as a "comer." Regardless of impact, your best interests lie in resisting the call of inactivity and doing something.

Doing something may or may not be an ethical matter. Certainly, the taxpayers or shareholders have a right to expect that you will not waste your time and their money, but it may also be a simple matter of self-interest not to let grass grow under your feet.

## Rule 71: Do the Right Thing—Carefully

You are quite likely to find yourself in situations that involve either doing the right thing or playing it safe.

My advice is to do the right thing, but do it carefully so that you can limit the damage to yourself. Doing right is always dangerous, but in the long run it is, after all, the right thing.

Maybe this story will make the point: A very competent mid-level program analyst was put on a project with another office. The project was a large conference to be managed by an outside contractor. At one of the first project meetings, the key person from the other office disparaged blacks and women, even using racial epithets. This was done in front of the contractor's project person, who was a woman and whose boss (not present) was black. The contractor person complained to my friend. The dilemma was what to do. If my friend had done nothing, she would have betrayed her own principles and let down the contractor's project manager. She chose to consult her own boss and then tell the agency director about it. While the director disapproved of what the other employee had said, he took no action directly but asked the offender's supervisor to take care of it. This resulted in calls to my friend, the complainant, accusing her of being a troublemaker. The main interest of the offender's supervisor was to defend his employee, right or wrong. Although the insensitive person was removed from the project, his attitude hadn't changed and his own supervisors tacitly supported his actions by attacking the complainer. This incident turned out backward: The insensitive lout who did wrong became a hero, and my friend, who did right, had made enemies and was called a bad employee. Nevertheless, the complainer did the right thing.

This kind of thing is all too common in government and the private sector. People who speak out for truth, who report offenders, and make mistakes known are often in trouble. Some supervisors would rather attack the messenger than solve the problem.

The ultimate example of this is the fate of legitimate "whistle-blowers." They often are punished because they expose waste, fraud, and corruption, as well as just plain stupidity. While admittedly it is sometimes difficult to distinguish between whistleblowers and disgruntled employees, the good boss can tell the difference.

You are likely to face ethical issues often. You may be asked to perform an illegal act, to lie, or to do something that is legal but wrong. You may be asked to cover up a mistake. Well, it is necessary in these situations to behave honestly even though it risks your own well-being. After all, there is no virtue in telling the truth when there is no penalty. Honesty is only hard when there is a downside.

You should be careful when doing right. Try hard not to offend people. Try hard to be tactful—even generous—and try hard to avoid being sanctimonious. But in the end it is better to do the right thing, even if it hurts.

One could hope that virtue is more than its own reward, and

that your peers, your boss, and others in the hierarchy above you will appreciate that. Your courageous act may earn you respect and more important assignments. However, this is an imperfect world and the odds are that doing right will just get you into trouble. Go ahead and do right, but be careful!

## Rule 72: Make Your Word Your Bond

One of the best things you can do for yourself and everyone else is to make your word your bond. Never default on a promise or a deal.

A lot of business is done orally. There already are a lot of memos, letters, and other documents. More paper would clog the system even worse, so a lot of business is conducted orally at meetings, in classes, at lunch, and—allegedly—on the golf course.

You will be asked often to agree to something or promise to do something or even to do something. If you agree to something, you must follow through.

Keeping one's word is more than a matter of honor, however. It also is a matter of doing business rapidly and conveniently. There is so much to be done that it is essential to communicate, negotiate, and operate quickly. Being able to trust your peers and bosses allows you to go ahead and do things without having them in writing. Knowing that your opposite number will keep his or her word allows you to move on your part of the job without having to put it in writing. The same thing goes for you. If you keep your word, you are part of the solution instead of part of the problem.

Just think how it would be if no one kept their word. Everything would have to be in writing. You would have to have written contracts on even the simplest things. In effect, you would have to litigate almost every action. This would indeed clog up the channels of communication and block progress. Things are bad enough already. The requirements for documentation are already mind-boggling. There is already a lot of covering one's rear end by writing memos, and this is with a high level of trust and reliability in an organization. If there were no trust, there could be no progress.

So my advice is to keep your word. Give it cautiously, but once you do, live up to your promises. If circumstances change and you have to recant, you are obligated to inform the others as soon as possible. Keeping your word may not make you popular, but it will gain you respect and trust.

# Rule 73: Never Leak Information

As a member of an organization, you have an obligation to safeguard its property. Information that you have because of your status is organizational property that must be safeguarded just like computers, typewriters, pens, paper clips, or other property.

The rules for safeguarding tangible property appear to be clear. You may misuse pens and paper clips, appropriate them for personal use, or even steal them for profit, but you at least know that you are committing a crime. That is, office workers know that it is wrong to take a government or company pen home for personal work even though some do it. Most workers may be able to rationalize that stealing a pen is so trivial as to be OK, but stealing a computer is wrong. The fact is that converting government or corporate property to personal use or for private gain is recognized as wrong by even the malefactors.

Many employees fail to recognize that information also is to be safeguarded.

The government wants to keep sensitive or classified information from unfriendly nations. Corporations want to keep proprietary information on their products and finances from their competitors. All organizations have information that they want to keep within their organization, consistent with the requirements of the law. Nevertheless, there is a sort of double standard about information that leads to leaks—particularly but not exclusively from the government. A leak is the clandestine revelation of information to an unauthorized person.

In order to understand the situation, it is useful to identify four basic kinds of leaks.

1. **The whistle-blower leak.** This is a leak of information to the news media concerning some illegal or negligent action by another employee or group or by the bosses. The point is to correct the improper situation. Presumably, the leaker has tried to correct the situation through official channels but has been rebuffed by authorities who want to cover up their negligence or criminality. The only recourse is to blow the whistle. Whistle-blowing is encouraged by law, and there is a special government agency to protect civil service whistle-blowers from retribution for having exposed the sins of their bosses. There have been some famous whistle-blowers who apparently have a special affinity for improper situations and expose them one after another in ever-ascending importance.

2. **The disgruntled employee leak.** This is a leak by an employee who has suffered some real or imagined injury. The employee may have been denied promotion, demoted, or even fired. Ideas offered by the employee may have been ignored. Credit for ideas that were adopted may have been stolen by a boss. The common thread is that the employee has a grievance against one or more bosses. To get even, the disgruntled employee reveals information or makes allegations embarrassing to the bosses. It is hard to distinguish between these kinds of leaks and legitimate whistle-blower leaks.

3. **The ego trip leak.** This is committed by an employee who wishes to show off just how important he or she is. The importance is based on knowing something that less important people don't know. The leaker also is demonstrating just how unreliable and untrustworthy he or she is. The recipients don't really care about this; they are only concerned with the information and will cater to egos as long as they get the scoop.

4. **The official leak.** This is a leak by a responsible person for official purposes. A big boss deliberately and with authority releases information informally to media contacts. The official leak is used to float trial balloons, get a jump on the competition, build public support, damage other programs by premature revelations, or just to jockey for position. Although official, these

leaks are just as bad as the other kinds, maybe worse. They set a bad example because their presumed official nature makes it easier for the whistle-blowers, disgruntled employees, and egotists to justify their own transgressions.

There really is no satisfactory leak. None does credit to the leaker. They only cause trouble. I can see a case for legitimate whistle-blowing, but I have to tell you that I find it hard to believe that a resourceful worker cannot obtain justice within the system. Perhaps I am naive. If so, whistle-blowing is necessary under some circumstances.

My advice to you, however, is to never leak information. Never succumb to the temptation to provide unauthorized information to unauthorized persons in a clandestine manner.

## Rule 74: Never, Never, Never Leak Classified Information

The rule about never leaking unauthorized information goes triple for information that has been classified CONFIDENTIAL, SECRET, or TOP SECRET under federal law.

Never, never, never leak classified information. In fact, don't even discuss it until you have verified personally that the other people have valid security clearances and have a need to know the information.

Many workers in the government and the private sector are authorized access to classified information. They work routinely with it. This sometimes creates an aura of nonchalance. One risk to security comes from sheer laxness by people who deal routinely with classified information. Fortunately, security offices are on to this and inspect enough to keep the situation under control.

Some people work mostly in unclassified areas. In these offices a classified document causes such a stir that security usually is well served, if communication is not. So intermittent contact with classified material can be handled.

The biggest security risk, aside from foreign agents, is the self-serving egotistical leaker. These employees look on classified information as a real status symbol. The fact that he is cleared for SECRET or TOP SECRET information is a big deal. It makes him more important than the unwashed and uncleared masses around him. In order to "enhance" his importance, he reveals classified information. This is really stupid. Not only does the leaker reveal himself or herself to be untrustworthy, but national security is imperiled.

Classified information is also leaked, apparently, by people who want to help or hinder a particular program. These people delude themselves by thinking that the crime is for a greater good. Fortunately, there are few of these ideological fanatics working in most organizations.

It is worth remembering that stealing classified information is a crime, and people who do it are criminals. In my opinion, people who receive stolen classified information—including journalists—are also criminals, the First Amendment notwithstanding.

My advice is to play it straight. Act in accordance with the laws, regulations, and security policy of your organization and safeguard classified information scrupulously.

# Survival Hints

In a large organization you can hurt yourself by what you do or do not do. You can do this without knowing it. Your actions and personality may cause you to be overlooked for promotion, denied the key jobs necessary for advancement, or even demoted or fired. So you need to take steps to protect yourself and survive.

You need to know where you really stand. One of the peculiar things about office life is that many employees have little idea of how they are regarded by their bosses or co-workers. Some of the most disliked employees appear to believe that they are the most beloved. Some of the worst bosses have no idea that their subordinates hate their guts. Many employees simply assume that they are doing a good job, and it comes as a great surprise when they are denied a promotion or transferred to a less important job. So the first general approach to survival is self-awareness. Look at yourself and what you do with objectivity and make an honest judgment on how well you are doing. This appraisal can help you really benefit from these rules.

I can't tell you how to avoid all of the bad things that can and do happen to good employees, but these general rules may help you survive and perhaps even flourish.

# Rule 75: If You Work Overtime, Show Results

Some workers are attracted to overtime, some are attractive to overtime, and still others have overtime forced upon them. So you will have the opportunity to work overtime at some point in your career. If you are an exempt employee, of course, you get to work overtime without extra pay. This is your reward for achieving "professional" level and working for an annual salary.

If you are lucky enough not to be exempt from overtime and holiday work laws, you will be paid handsomely for extra hours. The incentive appears clear enough to warrant no more advice, except to say, "Get all you can."

The real difficulty is with unpaid overtime. Most of us do this when forced to and for hot projects and other serious and time-urgent situations. We work overtime willingly and even enthusiastically for a while, then the flesh and spirit flag as a function of age and experience. The more overtime you put in, the less likely you are to want to do it again. So for most of us overtime is not thrilling.

A few workers love overtime, thrive on it, and seek even more of it. These people are known workaholics. Some of them have unhappy home lives, are lonely, or do not have other interests. Some are genuine fanatics who identify so closely with their programs that they sacrifice their personal lives for professional progress. These people are to be respected cautiously and watched carefully.

Some people put in overtime thinking that it is a way to impress the boss, gain promotions and bonuses, and get ahead in a cruel world. This is a risky course, for overtime is an input rather than an output. We are all aware of the difference between input, which is activity, and output, which is progress. Many of us have seen individuals or entire offices that showed great deal of activity without much progress. This general lack of output is tolerated during normal work hours. Some people even hypothesize that the function of an organization is to stifle change without seeming to do so. So it may or may not be necessary to actually produce something during normal work hours.

However, if you draw attention to yourself by working overtime, the situation changes. Voluntary overtime is an ostentatious display of ambition or advocacy, both of which are suspect. Thus, when you work overtime voluntarily, you will call attention to an unusual, even abnormal, level of activity. You will be expected to produce something.

So the general rule for overtime is that it has to be productive. When you work overtime voluntarily, you should produce a memo, a briefing, a document, or something to show that you did not just put in the extra time sitting around, talking on the phone, reading the newspaper, or doing the things you do during regular hours. Overtime is serious stuff.

This rule is particularly important to workers who make a fetish of odd hours. There are people who come in late and leave late. Some are high-level executives who apparently have difficulty getting up in the morning. These people show up at 10:00 A.M. and stick around until 7:00 P.M., presumably to impress the front office. Some workers with exotic specialties, such as computer programmers, really display odd hours. They come into the office in the afternoon and work, or pretend to work, all night.

These people can get away with this only if they produce something useful. I was in an office once where the young genius computer programmer flouted all the rules. He dressed funny, came to work late, stayed late, and spent a lot of time shooting the bull with other employees, keeping them from their own work. This was tolerated for a long time by the boss, who thought the young genius was actually creating critical software. When the deadline came, the program was not there, and the employee was fired. The point is that this employee would have been kept on if he had behaved normally. The job was tough, advanced, and risky. The required software program probably was too hard, so a conventional worker could have failed without penalty. The hotshot young genius set high standards for production by acting outside the normal rules and suffered the appropriate penalty when he failed to produce. So the best thing to do is to produce something when you work overtime and show it the next day.

# Rule 76: Don't Say Bad Things about Anyone

This rule is hard to follow, but it is prudent. It is tempting to bad-mouth other people. It is tempting to say insulting things about the boss, the boss's executive assistant, the boss's secretary, the division chief on the third floor, and everyone and anyone else. Sometimes the bad things are justified; most of the time they are exaggerated or based on parochial views and, thus, unwarranted. But whether the bad things are correct or incorrect is irrelevant. The real point is that it is terribly unwise to say them out loud.

One reason for this is that, invariably, people find out about it. If you confide in your trusted co-worker that Mr. X is a real louse, Mr. X will probably hear about it by the close of business that day. If you tell jokes about your vice president at the office party, he or she will be told about it at work the next day. So one reason to keep your mouth closed is because you live and work in a society in which it is impossible to keep gossip from flowing freely.

You cannot even safely bad-mouth subordinates, outgoing employees, or even born losers. You can never tell where the object of your scorn will end up. He or she might just show up as the assistant secretary four years later and be your Big Boss. It is not pleasant to work for a person whom you have insulted previously.

Saying bad things about other people is also very revealing about your own character. Your audience may laugh or giggle nervously at your clever, biting insults about co-workers or bosses, but they will also trust you less. If you bad-mouth others in their presence, they conclude that you probably bad-mouth them with the others. Your contempt for others lowers your own standing accordingly.

My mother once said, "Never say anything you would not want printed on the front page of the *New York Times*." That is particularly good advice when talking about other workers. If you can't say anything good, don't say anything. Above all, don't become an office bad-mouther.

# Rule 77: Say Good Things Only When They Are Deserved

Some bosses go overboard in trying to spread the credit or bond with their workers by praise. Having heard only part of Management 101, they go around lavishly praising people for everything and anything.

You have probably heard this or perhaps been subjected to it. You have done some work that is routine—good stuff, but nothing really more than what you do all of the time. The boss, feeling good that day or trying to make an impression on his or her boss, says how wonderful that job was and what a great report you submitted. This happens when bosses are making an overt try at winning the hearts and minds of their employees.

But, the boss who lavishes praise for routine work or, worse, for substandard work, is not going to win any hearts or minds. Employees are quite aware of the quality of their work. They know when the job is up to par, subpar, or really better than par. So the boss who praises substandard or average work is going to come across as a faker. Once a boss lies about something as basic as this, the workers never quite trust anything he or she says.

So my advice is to give praise to workers only when that praise is deserved. On the other hand, always try to give credit for really good work.

We have all heard about legendary executives who were sparing in their praise. As a result, workers scrambled to earn a whisper of "not bad" or "seems OK." These bosses sought to increase the value of praise by keeping it only for the very best work and by setting up a scale of praise, so that "outstanding" really meant that.

Rating systems depend on statements about the work of the person being rated. They start out with scales like "outstanding," "excellent," "good," "fair," and "poor." After a while the ratings tend to cluster at "outstanding." Many bosses are simply afraid to give an honest rating because they know that it could kill an employee's career. So almost everyone, except really bad employees, is rated outstanding. A rating of "excellent" is tantamount to failure. This praise inflation appears to skew any rating system ever devised, so you should be aware of the problem when praising your own workers.

My advice is to establish your own praise-rating scale. Decide on the words you want to describe certain qualities of work. If you are outgoing, you might adopt "truly outstanding" as your highest mark. A more conservative approach would be to use "very good" as the highest mark. It really doesn't matter much what you say as long as you are consistent in using your own praise scale. The workers will soon catch on to your system and know that "very good" is a really top rating.

The big point is that you lose a lot by giving praise when it is not merited. If lousy work is praised just as much as good work, there is no incentive to do better. You should avoid becoming known as a baloney artist who just shoots off your mouth to say something, even if it is wrong.

## Rule 78: Be Nice to Personnel

While it is generally good policy to be nice to *everyone*, it is particularly good policy to be nice to the personnel people.

Personnel people have both considerable power and considerable reluctance to use it for you. They appear to believe that they are the *real reason* that the organization exists. They give the impression that the substantive programs of the organization are only pretexts to support the really essential work of recruiting, hiring, classifying, promoting, and disposing of employees. If you disagree, just think of the last time that the personnel section helped you without your begging for it.

The inflated self-important attitude of personnel sections is greatest in the federal government, where rules take precedence over reason. Federal personnel rules are so dedicated to fairness that they become eminently unfair in application. There are so many rules that it is hard to apply all of them simultaneously without committing a misdemeanor. Thus, personnel people, who know the rules and keep that knowledge to themselves, have real power.

Personnel management in the private sector appears to be

less bound by rules (other than those imposed by the government), but it tends to be just as self-serving.

This application of power by the personnel people always seems to work to the disadvantage of the program offices. There are the usual attempts to reduce grades, obstruct simple reorganizations, and slow action on even the simplest changes. It is only when a supervisor wants to get rid of a poor employee that the full power and credit of the personnel system is engaged to protect the worker.

I once joined an organization in the throes of a massive reorganization. The personnel people there had just initiated a massive program to establish the reduction-in-force rules for every employee, and every position was being audited to "rejustify" every grade. So in the midst of this gigantic turmoil, with morale at the bottom, the personnel office was trying to reduce everyone's grade and set up rules for firing and downgrading. While top management thought their workers were working, the entire work force was sitting around worrying over their finances and the future.

One of the things that federal personnel people have done best recently is to hand out the annual furlough notices required by the continual struggle between the Executive Branch and Congress over the budget. The same system that can lose pay actions, misplace promotions, stall transfers, and delay reorganizations can put furlough notices in the hands of the potential victims with outstanding speed and efficiency.

Now this criticism of personnel systems is somewhat overblown, and I am sure that there are some good personnel people out there.

The rule is that an effective worker establishes and maintains good relations with the personnel office. This goes beyond merely a good professional relationship; effective damage control requires a warm and fuzzy relationship. If you go out of your way to thank the personnel people, invite them to the Christmas party, and beg, you may get service. Not better service, just basic service.

At any rate, it wouldn't hurt.

# Rule 79: Guard Your Turf

There is always so much talk about "turf" in the office that you would expect to see cattle grazing there. Turf is jargon for the activities under the control of a manager or executive. Turf includes the number and grades of the people in the organization and its office spaces, budget, and responsibilities. Responsibilities are the most important because they determine the number of subordinates, dollars, offices, desks, and computers under the purview of the manager. Accordingly, there is a lot of fighting about who is in charge of a particular issue, action, or project.

Turf fighting is good news and bad news. The good news is that people are actually fighting for the privilege of doing work—or a least being responsible for doing work. The bad news is that more time may be spent fighting over the work than in doing it.

Turf is important because the number of subordinates essentially establishes the title or grade—and thus pay—of a manager. The larger the number of people, the more likely it is that a promotion is in the cards. There are three kinds of turf fighters: the young pup, the mongrel, and the old dog.

Young pups are new guys who come in eager and ready to save the world. They often blunder into other people's turf in a kind of ignorant frenzy, tail wagging. In their eagerness to make progress and get things done, they inadvertently step all over other people's turf. These neophyte turf fighters are not very dangerous. After they run into an old dog or two, they tend to creep back to their own yard with tails between their legs. Nevertheless, they do cause a lot of fuss in their first full flush of territorial aggression.

Mongrels are dangerous. These are the ambitious and scheming kinds of turf fighters who deliberately plot to enlarge their turf. Since there is a fixed amount of turf available, the mongrel can expand only by taking it away from somebody. This causes a great deal of commotion, and the mongrels often win at first because they are underhanded. They often lose in the end for the same reason.

Old dogs are not interested in enlarging their turf. They are adamant about holding what they've got. They've generally been around a while and they have settled into a routine over which they have complete mastery. Their first goal is to protect their turf. All actions are scrutinized for impact on the home turf. Old dogs are vicious and generally defeat the mongrels.

The rest of us are just potential victims. Managers intent on doing their jobs often don't even know what hit them after a mongrel has taken away their analysis division or third-floor office suite. After one or two turf raids, a supervisor either becomes an old dog or abdicates the power struggle.

Make no mistake, turf is just a code word for power. The fight for turf is the fight to make, or influence the making of, policy. The real reward for most people is being in on the action.

This is what keeps many people working for the government. They want to be on the inside, know what is going on, and influence the action. Civil servants may not get paid as much as private-sector workers, but they believe that they have more power.

Turf fighting is here to stay. It is normal and as natural as apple pie and cheap handguns. My advice to you is to emulate the old dog. Don't try to get more turf at the expense of others, but defend your own to the death. If you are attacked, there are no holds barred. If you give up power under attack, you will rightfully be perceived by your tribe as a weak leader who cannot help his or her subordinates. That is the beginning of ineffectiveness.

## Rule 80: Look Out for the Dragon

Every Big Boss has a Dragon guarding the gate to the inner sanctum. The Dragon is listed on the organizational chart as the executive secretary or sometimes executive assistant, but he or she is really a Dragon.

The function of the Dragon is to keep unauthorized people from entering the Big Boss's inner sanctum and intruding on the sacred presence. They also monitor calls and even documents to assure that no authorized or unsavory material slips through.

Because of the nature of their work, Dragons have to act

mean and tough. Most of them are not really mean or tough but just act that way on the job. They have to be perceived that way even to get the job. Dragons have been known to smile, but never on the job. This is yet another of those tough jobs that has to be done by someone.

Do not think that you can gain access to the Big Boss by making friends with the Dragon. Dragons have no friends, at least not in the same office. They are permitted to breathe fire, issue smoke, and snarl and growl to do their jobs. This is in their job descriptions. So cringing and being obsequious to the Dragon are useless. Everyone cringes and is obsequious to Dragons.

I once had an outer office with one big Dragon and several smaller ones to protect me. One of the smaller Dragons had the job of reviewing every document that came to me for signature and nit-picking it. I mean catching every misspelling, dropped comma, and typo. She did a great job. That was the trouble. The workers and their branch chiefs and division chiefs would complain bitterly that Louise was a bottleneck and source of trouble. She may have been trouble for them, but she was a comfort to me. I knew that any paper processed by Louise was correct. I supported her completely. I used to ask her permission when I wanted to let a paper go out with a minor typo in order to beat a deadline. She was great and was doing exactly what I wanted and needed, though it did not make her very popular with the troops. To them, she was a Dragon. To me, she was a guardian angel.

The only people who can really intimidate Dragons are bigger bosses. Dragons have no real status but, like the moon, shine with the reflected light of their bosses. So when a really big sun shows up, it is the Dragon's turn to cringe and be obsequious. After this has happened, you should stay away from the front office for twenty-four hours, for Dragons really resent having to be nice.

It is no use telling the Big Boss about how mean and tough his Dragon is, for that is just what the Big Boss wants. The Big Boss does not want to be interrupted or meet with a bunch of people who will only waste his or her time.

But the Big Boss has to appear to be Mr. Nice Guy, so he or

she hires a Dragon to guard the gate. The Dragon gets all the blame and the Big Boss gets the freedom. If you get to be a Big Boss, the first thing you should do is get a Dragon of your own.

In the meantime, be nice. Even Dragons need to be loved.

## Rule 81: Follow Security Rules

In your organization there will be a lot of security rules. I mean a lot. You may have to check into the building. Check out of the building. Get up from your desk and meet visitors and check them in and out. Wear your badge. Show your badge. Account for documents. And all kinds of things that slow you down and occupy valuable time.

My advice is to follow these security rules scrupulously all of the time. Whether they make sense is not in your area of competence. The rules were invented by security professionals to guard the personnel, property, and information of your organization. They are responding to a threat whose dimensions are probably very vague to you. Just because you don't know much about the threat does not mean it is not there.

This is a dangerous world. There are threats from agents of foreign powers. Terrorists are sponsored by nations and supported by an international network. There are criminals, organized and working alone. There are gangs. There are special-interest groups whose advocacy has slipped over into fanaticism. There are unscrupulous competitors. There are many people and groups who threaten you and your work environment.

Security rules try to establish routines that reduce the risk to you, your co-workers, and your work place. The rules are designed to make it hard to steal products, equipment, and even office supplies, which is a big thing in some organizations. They are designed for your protection no matter how inconvenient they may seem. The right way to deal with these rules is to make obedience to them a habit.

Some people disobey security rules because they think the whole thing is silly. Some big shots believe that because they are big shots, they do not have to obey the same rules as the peasants.

Some peasants disobey the rules in rebellion. All of these people are wrong.

It is fairly easy to get around security rules if you want to. The system usually assumes that employees are responsible adults who will cooperate. The security system is designed to defeat outsiders. If insiders want to, they can beat the system.

My advice is to take security seriously. Play ball. Obey the rules and tell all of your peers and subordinates to do so. Don't second-guess the security professionals, and don't damage your agency and your work by thinking you are above it all.

## Rule 82: Maintain a Sense of Humor

The one indispensable trait of an office worker is a keen sense of humor. This is necessary for survival.

Life in an office can be crazy and unsettling. You may be at the mercy of an unstable boss. You can't get approval for your program. Personnel is going to desk audit your job. The budget has been cut again. Your last briefing bombed. The conference in Palm Springs has been canceled. Yet another project report is due tomorrow morning first thing. Sales are down for the third month. You haven't even written up the quarterly progress report, which won't report any progress. So there is a lot to be upset about.

Getting upset, however, is a self-defeating response to office adversity. It only serves to please your latent critics, who are hovering in the background waiting to say, "I told you Joe was going over the edge." It will upset your boss, who is probably having problems of his own. It will certainly upset your spouse, girl- or boyfriend, children, and co-workers. So overt anger, no matter how soothing it may be from a clinical viewpoint, is not a great response.

It is far better to find the humor in these situations. Believe me, if life is a comedy, working in an office is a whole evening at the Comedy Club. People are often funny under difficult circumstances, so the office and its foibles provide fertile ground for a humorous approach.

This pertains particularly to your own role. Don't take yourself so seriously. There is nothing worse than a stuffed shirt with no sense of humor. So keep some perspective and maintain a sense of humor about yourself, your work, and your relative importance in the great scheme of history.

My advice is to keep an eye open for the funny things. When the boss has gone bonkers again, think of King Kong. When your classifier shows up to prepare you for the downgrade, try to notice how funny he or she is. Ha, ha! When your briefing bombs, reflect wryly before doing it over. When the contract is awarded to a competitor, sing a funny song. When the budget is cut, cry into your beer until you laugh. When sales slump, tell jokes. If you try, you can find something funny about even tragic events, and you will have to do that to stay sane and effective in an office.

Of course, not every tragedy can be converted into comedy. Government and commerce are serious business, but they get deadly if taken too seriously. So it is best to leaven the burden with a layer of humor. If laughter is the best medicine, take a healthy dose each morning before work.

## Rule 83: Don't Make an Enemy Unintentionally

It is easy to make enemies in an office. Simply failing to return a phone call might be enough. Getting mad at the wrong time is likely to turn someone into an enemy. Cutting in on someone's turf is certain to make the other person into an enemy. Most of all, differing with someone on a matter of substance can make you an enemy.

Making enemies is part of the job, but you don't want to do it accidentally or naturally. You should only make an enemy intentionally and then only when the stakes are high.

You can avoid making enemies unintentionally by returning phone calls, remaining calm and courteous, and respecting other's rights, privileges, and turf. You can disagree with most people on matters of substance and still not make an enemy. You can do that by being courteous (even cordial), by listening as well as talking, and by avoiding emotional arguments. Attack the other worker's position; do not attack the other worker personally. I used to say, "It's OK to say that Brinkerhoff is *full* of baloney, but it's not OK to say that Brinkerhoff *is* a baloney."

If you avoid outrageous behavior, you will be able to pursue your policies and programs without making enemies of most people.

It is also true that you will make some enemies no matter how nicely you behave. Some of your fellows will hate you just because you oppose them on some matter of substance. These people have a problem, and it is not your problem. So just behave yourself no matter how badly the other party behaves.

There are times, however, when you will have to make an enemy in order to forward your goals. I am talking about your policy or program goals, not your career goals. If you care about what you are doing and are certain that you are right, it may be worth it to make an enemy to win your point. This is a risky business, however, and you should adopt such a course of action only after concluding, after sober contemplation, that no other course is open to you to achieve your policy goals and do your job.

This situation might arise, for example, if you decide that you have to contradict a peer at a meeting with your common supervisor in order to get a memorandum approved. If you do this, you will have humiliated your peer and most likely gained an enemy. The price you pay for short-term victory will be long-term lack of cooperation and some return shots at future meetings. You must be certain that this price is worth it.

Urgency might excuse deliberately making an enemy, but this is overrated. In large organizations urgency is not always the best policy. If urgency leads to making enemies either deliberately or accidentally, it ultimately is counterproductive. Better to pass up some little victories that would involve making enemies in order to advance your program in another way. This takes longer but is probably better strategy in the long run.

You will have enemies. That is not necessarily bad; people are known by the enemies they make. The best you can do is to try to have earned enemies, rather than the inadvertent kind.

# Rule 84: Have the Perks You Deserve

One benefit of working in a large organization is that you get perquisites as you move up the ladder of success. These tangible signs of seniority are called "perks."

Perks include the size and location of your office, furniture, the proportion of a secretary you can count on, and little things such as water carafes and desk sets. For more senior people, you can get an agency decal or corporate logo for your office. Senior government officials can have U.S. and agency flags in their offices. Finally, there are some really good deals, the ultimate of which is a blanket travel order allowing you to go when and where you please without asking anyone.

There are several ways to approach the gaining and possession of perks.

One way is to parade them as a mark of superiority. This is tacky and *nouveau riche.* Another way is to pretend indifference and disclaim any interest whatsoever in the tangible rewards of rank. This is phony for the most part; if genuine, it is so humble as to be inappropriate.

The only real way to treat perks is to accept them as your due and show obvious appreciation for them without boasting. They are something for junior employees to work for. They are the signs of success and are nice to have.

So you should always make certain that you get the perks appropriate for your grade and position. If you are sharp, you will know exactly the entitlements for each higher grade. When you get there, make no bones about arranging for your perks. Don't be bashful. Faint heart ne'er won the big policy fight. If you don't have the perks, your clout will be diminished, and clout is everything.

# Rule 85: Don't Agree to Anything in Haste

If you are going to keep your agreements, it is wise to avoid agreeing to anything foolish. That is easier said than done. There are many reasons for agreeing to foolish deals—pride, ignorance, desire to please, or misplaced self-interest. One of the biggest reasons for foolish agreements is simple haste.

Office life tends to be hectic. The placid scene masks a frenzy, at least for those actually working. It is true that some professionals read the paper leisurely and some secretaries do their nails at the desk. But most office workers actually work hard. For these the pace is fast and furious, generating tremendous time pressure.

A philosopher once said that all of the best things in life occur very quickly. It seems the more important the issue and the bigger the stakes, the less time is available. The $50,000 minor project languishes for weeks while the decision memo on the $100 million project has to be in the front office by close of business—or first thing in the morning.

So most workers are rushed. And this haste causes not only errors and miscalculations but also bad deals.

When the pressure is on and time is short, be very deliberate about what you do. Don't lose your cool. Be particularly vigilant about agreements you make under the pressure of deadlines. It is in these moments, when you are focusing entirely on getting the job done in time, that you are most vulnerable to making mistakes.

Draw back at the time when the pressure is most critical. Look at the work. Make a sanity check. Think about it! Is it correct? Is it good? Is it wise? You don't have to take all day; just take a few minutes to stop the frenzy and look again. This will save a lot of blunders.

In any case, keep in mind the motto of Pentagon workers: "You want it bad, you get it bad." Unfortunately, there is a lot of truth in that. Nevertheless, do what you can to make it good the first time, even if you know it will be coming back for more work. You never know when it will be sent forward for real.

# Other–Other–Other

A good friend who spent much time in the Army, the government, and private enterprise complained that he spent his entire career working on other-other-other projects. This comes from programs and budgets, in which important projects and line items are categorized. After the important projects are named, there are always a few miscellaneous items, or "odds and sods," left over. These are put at the end of the budget under "other." Within this category there is also an assortment of leftovers, again listed as "other." At the third level there are leftovers grouped under the heading of "other." It would be possible to carry this process out several more steps, but you should be able to grasp the idea.

"Other" items always have the lowest priority for money, people, equipment, and the attention of the front office. Important projects always have their own names and budget lines, so you can imagine what it must have been like for my friend to have spent his entire career working on other-other-other.

When I came up with some rules that did not fit well with any other rules, the Other-Other-Other chapter was born.

# Rule 86: Be Nice to Auditors

There are two general classes of people in an organization—those who do things and those who check up on those who do things.

The second group includes auditors, inspectors general, congressional staff members, employees of the General Accounting Office, the Office of Management and Budget, the Defense Contract Audit Agency, and most budget examiners. They all perform some auditing function by examining whether what other people have done makes sense, fits the rules, and can be financed.

Auditors are a necessary evil. They perform a dirty job. We tend not to like them because they catch us in our mistakes and they question things we believe are obvious. They force us to re-examine our basic assumptions, check our arithmetic, and face our own biases. They make us uncomfortable and, if they are good at their work, they make us mad.

I used to complain when I had three program people working on a project and eight GAO people investigating them. My humble goal was to reduce the questioner-to-questionee ratio to 1:1. We had to spend so much time explaining our project that we had no time to do it. These days there are too many auditing agencies and too many people looking over workers' shoulders. This is not the fault of the auditors; they are just following orders.

I had the privilege of attending the Federal Executive Institute, which educates senior executives of the career civil service. Each class includes executives from many agencies and jobs. This is purposeful and helpful. We were organized into seminars or working groups. One of the members of our working group was a high-level auditor who was a really nice guy and a capable professional. We all had to give a talk to the group and his talk was titled: "Auditors Need to Be Loved, Too." I confess that this was the first time I had thought of that, but it is true.

Large organizations grapple with great issues. That is their raison d'être. There is much to be done and not enough time and money to do it all. This forces competition for resources. Auditing measures how well we spend time and money, and the results of the audits provide corrections and influence future resource allocation. So auditing is necessary, and the best response is to have your act together rather than to be discourteous to the auditor who comes to review your programs.

Remember to be nice. That does not mean you roll over and play dead. Auditors have no more special access to wisdom than any other group. Moreover, because they criticize other people's work rather than doing original work, they tend to lack imagination and vision. Don't worry about this. A lineman doesn't need to be able to throw the football to be a valuable member of the team. An auditor doesn't need to be able to create a program in order to find a flaw in yours. So treat them as adversaries, which they are, but also with respect and civility. Your own program will be strengthened, your mind will be clearer, and your conscience purer.

## Rule 87: Use Words Carefully

A hallmark of any profession or field of knowledge is jargon. Jargon is a language containing terms that have special and unique meaning for people in a particular field.

Many people disapprove of jargon and try to stamp it out. I like it. Jargon facilitates communication among members of a group because it functions as a kind of shorthand. An expert can use a term that has a precise, subtle meaning with the confidence that his listeners will understand exactly what he means. This is very useful.

People who complain about jargon are mostly outsiders who don't understand what is being said. This is perfectly understandable. So members of special groups or professions have to be careful when communicating with outsiders. Some insiders like to flaunt their jargon in front of innocent outsiders. This is rude and arrogant.

You have developed a jargon that you use in your office, company, agency, or profession. You and others like you have developed words, phrases, and (above all) acronyms that stand for concepts, systems, models, programs, and elements. You know what is meant by your jargon. Keep in mind that others probably do not.

You should use jargon freely within the group. Its power to transmit exact shades of meaning is good. My advice, however, is to avoid the use of jargon with people outside your group. This will decrease confusion and may increase comprehension. It may be difficult to use lay language to describe subtle concepts. You may indeed be unable to express your special knowledge without jargon. This is normal.

The answer is to use words carefully. I believe that each word in the American language has an exact, unique meaning. American is a complex language with many apparent synonyms that aren't synonyms at all when examined closely. Every little word turns out to have a meaning all its own. If you believe this, you should try to exercise some discipline when using words. Do not use two words for the same idea interchangeably. This will confuse outsiders who may not appreciate the substitution. Do not use jargon expressions confusingly.

Words are very important and you should treat them well. Polish them. Use them carefully and they will convey your ideas clearly and succinctly.

## Rule 88: Avoid Talking to the Media

Unless you are a professional public relations person or a big boss, my advice is to avoid talking to or having contact with the media—journalists, TV people, and writers of all sort.

Dealing with the media is like handling the big cats at the circus. You have seen it. The animal trainer goes into the cage with the lions, tigers, and leopards. The audience believes that the trainer knows what to do, but there is enough doubt to make it thrilling. And once in awhile the cats become unruly, forget their training, and hurt a trainer.

Media people are like the big cats. They are inherently dangerous. They have lots of clout and sometimes forget the rules of civilized behavior. And some of them are bad animals.

None of us would enter that cage at the circus without a lot of training, experience, pay, and insurance. Why would we want to deal with the media with less protection?

Most large organizations hire professionals to take care of public relations. The government surely does. Many corporations do, and the others should. The public relations staff deals with the press, radio, TV, and any other media that want to know and publicize what is going on in your agency. These professionals know—or claim to know—how to do this without getting themselves or the organization into trouble. Let them do it.

Big bosses have to deal with the media as part of their job. Interviews for publication or TV help put forth the organization's facts and opinions. The big bosses have to do this. Some are better than others, but all are supported in this by their professionals. It is a risky job, but they have to do it. Let them do it.

Some workers believe they can tangle with the media and benefit. They are naive. The media will eat them up. An inexperienced person will give away secrets or blast company policy within minutes after falling into the clutches of an investigative reporter. Or, the person will get angry and insult the reporter. Either way, the organization loses and the worker has hardly put another gold star on the record for that pay period.

So let me make it clear. Unless you are paid to mingle with the minions of the media, don't. Leave this hazardous and unrewarding task to the professionals and the politicos.

## Rule 89: If You Talk to the Media, Tell the Boss

You may have to talk to the media sometime even though you don't want to. You might want to do it despite my advice against it. In either case, you should inform your boss immediately of any contact with the media.

You are always representing your organization, during work hours or after. You cannot speak as a private individual. You cannot separate your private life from your work existence. This is just as true in the private sector, by the way, as it is in the public. If you are part of an organization, you are assumed to represent it. (If you don't agree with the organization, get out of it!)

So your words will be taken seriously by the media person with whom you have made contact. If you criticize your organization, it will show up as the views of a disgruntled employee. If you expose a secret, it will show up as a leak. If you state an opinion as to what ought to be done, it will show up as company policy. So it is hard to win when talking to the media.

There may be occasions, however, when you will run into a reporter or TV person and cannot avoid saying something. You may be incautious enough on those occasions to say a few words about business. You may speak in the heat of argument or advocacy. You may regret making those statements the next morning.

If this happens, you need to take immediate action to limit the damage to you and your organization. The way to do this is to consult your boss. Tell the boss that you had contact with a media person and that you said this or that or responded this way or that way. This lets him or her know the extent of the problem. If the incident is trivial, that will be sufficient. If the incident is serious, it may call for informing the big boss and the public affairs professionals. The first step for you is to tell your boss what you have been up to.

Am I paranoid about this? Possibly, but even if I am paranoid about the media, it is unwise to deal with them on behalf of the government or a corporation unless you know what you're doing. If you do slip, you are obligated to report that as soon as you can.

## Rule 90: Avoid Perfection

One of the most important rules is to avoid trying to do your work perfectly. If you try for perfection, you will accomplish less. This is summarized in the old saying, "The best is the enemy of the good."

I once worked with a midlevel professional who really tried to write perfect papers. The rest of us would write a draft, edit it once or (if we were really serious) twice, then run it up the chain of command for approval. This guy would not do that. He would tool and re-tool that paper for hours and days. This was before computers, and he would do it in longhand. He went through a dozen or more doublespaced drafts, with finely written changes on the margins of each. When he finally finished the paper, it was really good. Each word was a polished gem. Each sentence was crystal clear. Each paragraph, a solid rock. He took so long to do these perfect papers, however, that he was always late, always overtaken by events, and so unproductive that they fired him. Sic transit!

It is a property of the learning curve that when you start a project, you get a lot of output for a little input. As you progress, you get less and less output for each additional increment of input. At some crossover point you get less additional output for an equivalent additional amount of input. As you continue to work, the additional output produced for an increment of input gets very small. This occurs on the flat part of the curve. It is wise to stop adding input when you get there.

In other words, it is much more efficient and productive to achieve 95 percent of perfection than to try to get to 100 percent. In theory, you cannot reach perfection. As you approach it, the incremental cost gets huge. This phenomenon is well understood by some. It is unknown apparently to many managers who insist on perfection by their workers. The Army at one time had a major program calling for "zero defects." This was a major mistake. Such striving is certain to cause frustration and waste in an attempt to attain the unattainable.

This does not mean that you should settle for poor work. On the contrary, you should continue to strive to improve the quality of your work. But improve a little bit at a time so it doesn't become overwhelming. Keep on improving until you know that the effort is too great for the potential payoff. You will be approaching the flat part of the learning curve. You will also be providing high quality for a reasonable cost.

So my advice to you is, first of all, to understand the concept so that you can feel comfortable with less than perfection. I am not advocating that you do less than your best; just that you apply some common sense when you define "best." Then set for yourself reasonable standards of performance that you can achieve with a reasonable expenditure of resources. This should put you up high on the learning curve almost to the flat part and allow you to turn out good work rapidly with enough time and energy left for the rest of your work.

## Rule 91: Don't Get Mad

The best advice I can give anyone is don't get mad. Life is too short.

I am talking about mad mad, not crazy mad. It is not good to go crazy, either, but that is not the topic for this rule.

Working in an office is frustrating and difficult, particularly if you care about what you are doing and want to accomplish something useful.

There will be great opportunities to get mad. You will find it no problem at all, if you are so inclined, to get mad at almost everyone and everything. You will probably have good cause—things will be bad. You will be treated poorly, others will not recognize your worth, and some may even steal your work and parade it as their own.

However, getting mad rarely solves the problem or erases the provocation. Getting mad has the universal effect of getting others mad. So one very good reason for not getting mad is because it is simply not an effective way to get your work done.

Getting mad takes a lot of energy that could be used better, and that angry kind of energy is never directed at doing good.

Getting mad is thought by some to be worthwhile self-expression—sort of a therapeutic act. I doubt this. While screaming may make you feel good, it seldom wears well on your co-workers. You get mad and they really don't like it. It also gets to be a habit. You may not even notice how easy it is to slip out of control. Once you do it a few times and you think it makes you feel better, you tend to do it again. That kind of habit will turn you into a curmudgeon.

One of the worst things about getting mad is that it means that you have lost control of yourself. When you are in a white rage, you really don't know what you are doing or saying, and you may do things that you will regret. In any case, getting out of control is not healthy, and it certainly is not the mark of a solid worker.

If you decide not to get mad, you can still care. It is just that you channel your enthusiasm and drive more effectively. Anger is negative and destructive. Caring is positive and constructive.

You may have a hard time with this. If you tend to get angry, try some tricks to avoid exploding. Some people leave the room when they get angry; this has the advantage of avoiding unpleasant exchanges, but is does mark you as an angry person. It is better to restrain yourself and either say nothing or converse in low, modulated tones in a civil manner. Civility is the lubricant of communication. Few people like to converse with angry people; everyone likes to be treated civilly. If you can rise from civility to courtesy, so much the better. If you have really been provoked, cordiality may be too much. But avoid getting mad. It is, after all, a sign of weakness.

If, after all of this, you still get mad, at least do not show it. Showing anger is bad. Learn how to control yourself.

I am not just advising you to avoid showing anger. That is the first step, but real self-control comes when you can avoid being angry altogether. This is not easy. I am very sensitive to slights to my pride, and I "get hot" when treated rudely or insensitively. Nevertheless, it is better to stay cool and calm. That is the best way to make your point and to set the example of how to behave.

Anger is not only not necessary for passion, it is antipassion.

# Special Advice
# for Feds

This chapter consists of six rules that apply specifically to career federal civil servants. Most of the rules apply equally to public- and private-sector employees because all large organizations tend to be remarkably similar, but specific rules differ in the environments in which large organizations operate.

Much of my own time was spent in the Army (twenty-nine years) and the career civil service (nine years), so I know some of the special conditions for federal employees. These six special rules are just for them.

I have to tell you about the term "fed." It is a slangy name for a federal employee, and not too complimentary, either, in most usages. I ran across it for the first time when I was attending a governors' conference several years ago as a civilian official of the Department of Defense. When I got up to make a presentation before a committee of governors, I was referred to as a "fed." That stunned me. My idea of a fed was Eliot Ness (really Robert Stack) in "The Untouchables." I had no idea that state and local officials referred to us as feds. Anyway, as a catchy title for this chapter, I used "fed" to mean all of you federal employees.

Federal employees have special attributes. They get paid whether they work or not. For all practical purposes, they cannot get fired for poor work, though a few are fired each year for cause. They can get fired or furloughed because of budget cuts or budget fights. They do not work toward a "bottom line," which is to say they have no profit motive. They have tremendous impact on the lives and livelihood of all Americans and a lot of people in other countries, too. Finally, they have to work in an incredibly large and complicated organization whose top management consists of 535 chief executive officers.

Such special attributes call for a few special rules.

## Rule 92: Be Nice to Your Customers

You may think that this is strange advice. You work for the government, and you probably think that you don't have any customers. Wrong!

As a federal employee you have many customers, some of whom are far away and some of whom come into daily contact with you. If you work for the government, that means you work for all of the people of the United States. This probably sounds corny, but it is true.

Your customers are the people who are touched by or are subject to your programs. They include farmers, poor people, students, the homeless, union members, soldiers, sailors, airmen, marines, truck drivers, machinists, pilots, lobbyists, corporation executives, Native Americans, blacks, browns, and even WASPs. Because the federal government is so big and interacts in so many ways with people's lives, it is fair to say that all Americans are your customers.

The maxim that the customer is always right applies to the public sector as well as to the private. The private sector understands this because it has to sell products or services. If the customers are offended, they will not buy. Even so, there are numerous inexcusable examples of private-sector workers who become so entrenched that they become discourteous or unresponsive to customers. This kind of behavior by employees can have a direct and adverse impact on company sales because customers in the private sector can switch to another company whose employees provide better service. But we United States citizens cannot switch to another government if we are dissatisfied with the one we have. We have to stick it out until the next election. But even voting the rascals out does not always get rid of rude and indifferent civil servants.

So your first responsibility is to respond to letters, telephone calls, and face-to-face visits in a courteous and responsible manner. Too often we hear about government employees who are rude and unresponsive to citizen inquiries. Too often we hear about petty bureaucrats who think they are big shots and lord it over the humble citizens who must deal with the government. Too often we hear about citizens who have to fight for their entitlements through a maze of official indifference and opposition. Hey, it is your job to help the citizens, not fight them.

So make it a point, first of all, to be courteous. Even if you have to say no, say it pleasantly. Then try to be responsive. This means returning calls, living up to your promises, and knocking yourself out to get back to a person in trouble.

Next, be helpful. You know the rules. Chances are the poor citizen who needs your help doesn't have the faintest idea what is going on. Instead of using this situation to demonstrate your superiority, use it to help.

This is particularly important when citizens try to get into the system by calling high places. The higher you are, the more important it is to be courteous. Be just as attentive to the citizen's call as to the assistant secretary's call.

Remember who pays your salary. Act accordingly.

## Rule 93: Learn to Deal with Congress

There are three branches of the federal government. Most of you work for the Executive Branch. This includes the Office of the President, the Cabinet agencies, and the numerous independent agencies, boards, and commissions. A few of you work for the Judicial Branch. Some of you may work for the Legislative Branch as staff members for congressmen or congressional committees, the General Accounting Office, the Library of Congress, or other agencies within the Legislative Branch. This rule is addressed to employees of the Executive Branch.

There is great tension between the Executive Branch and Congress. This was the intent of the Founding Fathers as they structured the government. They had in mind that no single branch would dominate if there were a balance of powers among three elements. They wanted conflict within the government, and they got it.

There is no escaping Congress. It reviews your budget proposals and gives you part of what you asked for. It tells you what to do and how to do it. It then criticizes the way you do it. It employs hordes of auditors, analysts, and investigators with unspecified, sweeping powers who question you and your people and interfere with your work. If you don't do right according to Congress's views, it calls you to testify and grills you in public. It has all the cards.

So it is natural that many Executive Branch employees dislike and fear Congress. Most of this antagonism is toward the staffs. Most federal workers respect the elected representatives and believe in democracy. They do not believe that unelected congressional staffs should have so much authority and so little accountability. They resent some staffer giving orders and plunging around in their programs, pushing a personal agenda with the backing of a congressman. The Founding Fathers never expected this part of the rivalry.

Relax. There is nothing you can do about it. Congress knows very well what it is doing by expanding its bureaucracy. It will never go back to smaller or less aggressive staffs. It will not curtail the ever-increasing power of its own watchdogs—the General Accounting Office, the Congressional Research Service, and the Congressional Budget Office. Any expectation that Congress would cut its overhead and be easier to deal with if it just knew how bad it was for the poor Executive Branch is fantasy. This situation, however you regard it, is here to stay.

The only thing to do is to learn how to deal effectively with

Congress. If this means sucking up to insufferable staffers and massaging their enormous egos, so be it. These practices also have been known to exist within the Executive Branch, after all. You will just have to learn to treat staffers like you would treat any other demigod. Good luck!

## Rule 94: Be Nice to the Chairman of the Appropriations Subcommittee

Every bureaucrat learns quickly who the important people are in his life. Besides his bosses, these people are not always self-evident. The importance of people is always relative to what you want. You will find it wise to be nice to the personnel officer who grades the spaces in your branch. The guy in charge of computer repair might be important. The person who processes building passes and passports might be the one. There are a lot of people to whom it pays to be nice.

There is no one to whom it is more important to be nice than the chairman of the appropriations subcommittee for your agency. In the Senate, but particularly in the House of Representatives, this is the person who controls the lifeblood (money) of your agency. Your secretary, administrator, or director proposes, but Congress disposes. It tells your agency how much money you can have and it tells you how to spend it. The amount and the degree of direction your agency receives depends to a great extent on the good will of the chairman of your appropriations subcommittee.

The business of the federal government is too big for any individual or group to grasp. This includes Congress. Congress has to specialize in order to function. That means that there is no senator or representative who knows all about everything. There are, however, many senators and representatives who know a lot about specific programs or agencies. They specialize. They also have lots of help from personal and committee staffs.

Congressional staffs have grown tremendously in recent years. They are the real power behind the government. While senators and representatives remain in charge, the sheer work load and detail involved in legislation and appropriation mean that staffers are relied on more and more for answers. So every bureaucrat knows to be nice to the staffers who cover his or her agency. The staffers know this and get to be insufferable in their power and perquisites. There is no cure for this.

The really key legislator is the one who hands out the money. This is why the appropriations committees are a prized assignment. The chairmen of appropriations committees rule as emperors over vast domains, exercising power through viceroys (the subcommittee chairmen).

The real work of appropriations is done in the appropriations subcommittees. This is where the rubber hits the road, fiscally speaking. And this is why the chairman of the appropriations subcommittee for your agency is such an important person to you.

I know of a small independent agency whose administrator became overconfident and challenged the chairman of the appropriations subcommittee. The administrator went out of his way to antagonize the chairman. He was punished for this. The agency budget was cut, and the agency was severely constrained in spending what was left. The agency went into a tailspin, the administrator finally left, and his successor inherited the ill will and shrunken budget. It took years to get that agency and its programs back on track.

So my advice is to be nice to the chairman of the appropriations subcommittee for your agency.

# Rule 95: Treat Contractors as Part of the Team

Your office will always have more work to do than the employees can accomplish. This is partly just the nature of the beast, but it is also because the people who give you the work are not the ones who give you the resources to do the work.

Your agency's budget and work force are always being cut. Once in a while you might be lucky enough to get in an agency that is in a big buildup. Those are glorious times, but they occur seldom enough to warrant being classified as miracles. The norm in government is reduced rations and more work.

One of the perennial problems is shortage of staff. This is because the money for pay and allowances are often "fenced" from other funds and kept low by a watchful OMB and a suspicious Congress. The conventional wisdom is that there are too many fat bureaucrats doing nothing but living high off the taxpayer. While this may be true in other agencies or even in other offices in your agency, it is never true of your office. You will always have too few people to do the work.

One of the things that the government has done to get around this permanent state of understaffing is to create an entire industry in the private sector to do the work you can't do. Because the government has more work to be done than can be done in-house, large numbers of contractors have been formed to help you.

There has been a lot of bad press about government contractors, and defense contractors in particular. There has been some corruption, and there are always allegations of overcharging and bad work. Some of these bad things are true, but most contracting companies and employees are good people trying to do a good job.

As far as you are concerned, the status of the entire government contracting industry is not really relevant. You are interested in how well the contractor that supports you will do. Will the arrangements for your conference be made well? Will the new integrated computer system work the way you want? Will the study that you need to support your program be good work? These are important to you, and you can influence how well the contractors do.

There is an unfortunate tendency today for an adversarial relationship between government officials and government contractors. The reasons for this poor working climate are numerous, but they come primarily from the ever-stricter price competition in awarding contracts. The necessity for apparent fairness has spawned devices to get around the rules as well as penalties for government workers who are too friendly with contractors. Having good relations with contractors has been twisted into something evil, and being friendly with them is no longer permitted. The rules of the procurement process have unfortunately worked their way into the work place. So most government workers feel constrained in their relationships with contractors, and some have become hostile.

I have attended meetings where bureaucrats spoke of the "dirty contractors" and where contractors have been excused from the room peremptorily even though they had valid security clearances. I have seen government contracting officers and technical representatives treat contractors like dirt. Some government employees are starting to act as if contractors were enemies.

This unfortunate attitude has been reinforced by some dumb remarks by high officials about how bad the consultants and contractors are. There were also dumb actions that cut off funds and stopped contract awards for long periods without any discrimination or rationale. These arbitrary actions by a few high government officials reinforce the hostility felt by many in the bureaucracy toward contractors.

That attitude is just plain foolish. Where would the government be without contractors? Where would your office be without contract support? You cannot get along without them, so you should learn how to get the most out of them.

Contractors are people just like anyone else. Many of them, in fact, served in the government or the armed forces before they become contractor employees. That is where many of them learned the skills and gained the experience that make them so valuable in doing the government's work. Almost all are trying to do a good job. They would do a better job if you treated them like a member of the team instead of as an enemy.

The best contractor support I ever had when I was in government was on a hot project that needed some quick basic research to support important congressional testimony. I drew up a statement of work and sent it to a firm I knew could do the job. Two weeks later a sole-source contract was awarded and the contractor team was on the job. From the first I treated the contractor team as an extension of my staff. I assigned a supervisor to oversee its work, and I scheduled frequent meetings. We treated the contractors as if they were our own. The contractor people were good and did an outstanding job, on time, at cost, and saved the day for our office. Their work established a firm basis for an important program, and I used their report as a principal basis for my testimony. (The new contracting rules won't allow the quick award of any contract, particularly on a sole-source basis, so this kind of help is no longer available to program managers.)

I believe that one of the reasons we got such good results is that the contractors were taken into our group and made to feel a part of our team. As a result, they tried extra hard. The basic rule is to use every resource when you have a job to do. Contractors are resources, and they are people. Treat them well and they will treat you well.

# Rule 96: Avoid Getting Involved in Contracts

This bit of advice is for employees other than contracting officers. Contracting officers have to get involved in contracts because that is their particular niche. They get paid for it, and many are good at it despite all of the funny rules and constraints on procurement.

We all know that government procurement does not work well. The horror stories are told with increasing frequency. It takes longer to get a contract through than before. The process is difficult and not always successful. The contracts sometimes displease the program office sponsoring the work. The costs are often overrun. The products or services are too often unsatisfactory. This occurs everywhere in government, although the Department of Defense gets the most publicity.

No one knows how to fix the contracting mess. Every few years an idea pops up and becomes the fad. This has ranged for "fly-before-buy" to "buying-while-trying." The latest rage is "total quality management." Nothing seems to work. The situation is getting worse.

My personal opinion is that rigid insistence on price competition is a large part of the problem. Price competition is a procurement process in which bids are requested for a product or service and the low bidder wins. Most people think that this is good, but I do not. Price competition is OK when you are buying a simple product that can be specified exactly. Then you can get equal quality at the lowest price. When it is hard to estimate quality, as in a study contract, a developmental fighter, or a new computer system, price competition is not good. This book is not about problems in procurement, but I wanted to get that off my chest.

The fact is that with increased emphasis on competition, things have gotten worse instead of better. Someone should catch on that price competition is the problem instead of the solution. It would not be the first time that the conventional wisdom was wrong.

In olden days physicians thought that patients could be cured by bloodletting. So the doctors would attach leeches to the patient and take some blood. When the patient inevitably got worse (from lack of blood, if nothing else), the solution was to call for more leeches. When the patient died, the physicians all said, "We should have taken more blood." It is the same with price competition. Every time the procurement system takes a turn for the worse, the experts cry for more price competition.

The point for you program-oriented workers is that you should not get involved in contracts. It is being handled for you, and you will not be welcome. The fact that your programs and your dollars are at stake is irrelevant in today's procurement climate. The emphasis in procurement today is on process rather than product. The days when a program manager could get a $100,000 study contract under way in two weeks are gone, maybe forever. Today it would take most of you a year to get that study started. It takes five to seven years to get a major systems integration program, which dooms most offices to using old stuff forever. The procurement process is not going to get better, so you will have to plan accordingly. Figure on lead times over a year for new starts. In the meantime use the various devices that clever people have invented to get their work done in spite of the procurement process. I won't tell you what they are. That is another book. If you are worth your salt, you already know.

My advice is to steer clear of the contracting process. You can only get accused of conflicts of interest, breaches of the rules, or worse—trying to get something done quickly. Just relax and enjoy it!

# Rule 97: Defer to Political Appointees

If you are a career civil servant, you have an opinion about the political appointees who are over you. It's probably a poor one and may very well be justified.

Many political appointees are not as knowledgeable as careerists about their subjects. Many have had little or no experience in government and are more arrogant than their capabilities would justify. A few are hacks rewarded just for helping out in the campaign.

Of course, many political appointees are superb. They are experienced, capable, and knowledgeable. They fit in well and inspire their career staff personnel to greater things.

Judgments about political appointees are determined to a great extent by his or her attitude toward career civil servants. Many political appointees come into office regarding the civil servants with great suspicion. While there is some anxiety about the capability of the civil service, most of the suspicion concerns the political bias of the careerists. Republicans come into office believing that the civil service is full of radical left-wingers. Democrats come into office believing all civil servants are reactionary right-wingers.

As a result, political appointees tend to come on strong and shove aside civil servants, particularly senior ones. They fear that career employees, having a vested interest in previous programs, will oppose efforts to change the direction of government policy. Because they fear opposition, the political appointees prefer to bring in their own people—other political appointees—and to grade people according to their fealty to the ideology of the administration.

Since the political employees act this way, many career civil servants react adversely. They tend to oppose the politicals covertly and cause friction. They provide reasons why changes cannot be made instead of helping make the changes. They subvert and slow down the new leadership. This may be a natural response, but it merely tends to reinforce the political appointees' belief that the civil service cannot be trusted.

Both sides are wrong. The career civil service will serve loyally and well if given half a chance. Political appointees must show that they trust and rely on the career civil servants. Given this kind of leadership, the careerists will respond with enthusiastic support. Everyone likes to be liked, but no one likes to be liked more than civil servants.

On their part, the career civil servants have to stop fighting the problem, and they have to stop being the problem. They must defer to the political appointees. They must do this even to the meanest, most incompetent, most suspicious, and most downright ornery political appointee. It might not be easy, but it should be done.

Our democracy answers to the people's will. It may do this imperfectly, but it does it. Every four years we elect a president, and he gets to appoint his people to the political jobs throughout the Executive Branch. This is how the policies chosen by the people are put into effect.

If the people want it, the career civil servants have no right to oppose it out of personal belief. Though a particular political appointee may not articulate the people's will very well, he or she is entitled to presume that he is following the president's wishes. Accordingly, the career civil servant must defer to political appointees on policy.

It goes even further. The civil servant owes it to the people to do all that can be done to see that the policy is followed, even if he or she finds it repugnant. The civil servant must speak honestly about problems and pitfalls with the implementation of policy; he owes it to his political masters. He must do the best he can to establish programs that will carry out the policy.

# Perspective

This final chapter will help you keep a proper perspective on who you are and what you are doing. This is the uplift chapter and you may skip it if you are fed up with uplift. On the other hand, you might just benefit from these rules.

## Rule 98: Provide Support If That's Your Job

There are three general kinds of offices in any organization: program (or line), staff, and support. Program offices do the substantive work of the organization; they manage the projects and do the work for which the agency exists. Staff offices help program offices by performing certain specialized functions such as public affairs, quality control, or congressional relations. Support offices provide the essential services that allow the program offices to function. This rule pertains to employees in support offices.

Support offices cover such functions as personnel, payroll, facilities maintenance, cleaning, procurement, contracting, supply, accounting, security, and parking. All of these are absolutely essential to the proper functioning of an organization. Without them nothing could be done. Nevertheless, support functions are not the reason organizations exist. The program offices are. Without program offices the support offices would not exist.

The problem is that in many organizations the support offices have forgotten their role. They appear to believe that the organization exists for them. And they act like it. The personnel office believes that personnel is the most important thing and provides support to the program offices reluctantly, if at all. The comptroller people believe that the agency exists to provide quarterly reviews and budget justifications. The facilities people look on the program offices as people who abuse equipment and dirty the toilets. The security people see their function as the most important of all—providing security even if it means no progress. Now, some of these statements may be slightly hyperbolic, but every worker has run into support people like that.

This is based on personal experience that, to say the least, was disappointing. As a Big Boss at an agency I received VIP treatment. Getting a security pass was a treat, and everyone was unfailingly polite and helpful. When later I came back to that agency as a consultant, things were different. Although some people were courteous, as just another member of the public, I saw how it really was. And it was neither polite nor efficient. Processing was haphazard; the people did not seem to know what to do and were in no hurry to do it. It was a different experience for me, but probably all too common for most employees.

My advice to you people in support offices is to remember that you are there to provide service to the program offices, positively and politely. It is your sole job. If they call, you should jump. You should go out of your way to be helpful, responsive, and positive. You should take a proactive role by filling out forms yourselves instead of just sending them down to the program offices to be filled out by the workers there. When a program office wants to get something done, you should find ways to do it instead of finding reasons why it cannot be done.

It may be tough being in a support function—like being the

water boy on the football team. It is much more fun being a star who actually sets policy and implements programs. So it is perhaps natural that support office people would magnify their own importance to avoid a feeling of inferiority. It is also inexcusable to put one's pride ahead of accomplishing the organization's mission.

I was an Army engineer officer. Engineers are combat support troops, and we know it. It is our job to support the infantry, armor, and artillery, who are the stars of the battle and defeat the enemy. In combat, engineers assist the movement of our forces and impede the movement of the enemy forces. We engineers took pride in our combat support role. We never thought for a moment that the battle was fought just so we engineers could do our thing. Workers in support offices should emulate the engineers in this respect by taking pride in providing support to the program offices.

# Rule 99: Stop Complaining

One of the constant noises in an office is complaining. People complain about the job, gripe about the bosses, carp about the regulations, and put down the competition. You have only to hang around an office for a short time to hear the complaints.

Admittedly, there is something to complain about. Budgets are always insufficient. Congress is seldom satisfied. Sales go up and down. There is always more work than can be done. Some people don't appear to be carrying their share of the burden. The office is always being reorganized. People are always being moved. Bosses are seldom paragons. And so on, and so on.

We used to say in the Army that a little griping was a good sign, that it meant healthy morale. I am not certain about that. It seems that complaints are often based on dissatisfaction rather than contentment, so I take complaints seriously. They often are the visible sign of deep problems.

Nevertheless, my advice is to stop complaining. If you complain all of the time, it turns into whining. It also loses its value as a warning of a problem and becomes instead a symptom of deep malaise.

No one likes a chronic complainer. You know the type. Nothing is good, ever. Everything is insufficient and wrong. Since you can't please a chronic complainer, people stop trying. Don't be a chronic complainer.

Anyway, what have you got to complain about? You get paid well for working in an office. You have a lot of freedom on the job compared to most workers. You have great benefits and some job security. Anyway, if you don't like where you work, you can always quit.

If there is a real problem, see your boss. He or she gets paid to solve problems, real or imagined. But stop complaining about life in general. Nobody likes listening to it, and you hurt yourself without helping solve the problem.

My advice is to take a positive, or at least neutral, attitude at the office. Don't look at everything through rose-colored glasses—that would be insincere and just as bad as complaining—but recognize that as bad as your organization may be, it is also pretty good.

## Rule 100: Try to See the Forest Once in a While

We all know about Tree People and Forest People, from the old saying about "not seeing the forest for the trees." This brings out the truth that people who are involved in details often do not understand what they all mean. Tree People work on parts of the puzzle while Forest People comprehend the situation as a whole.

There are very few Forest People. Almost all of the bureaucrats I know are Tree People. Some are working on big trees, but still on one tree.

The scientific name for this tree person stuff is suboptimization. This refers to creating a really great solution for part of the overall system. Many people are suboptimizing and creating great solutions for all of the various parts of the system. The difficulty comes when the parts are put together (integrated!) and the whole thing does not work very well. The idea is that suboptimization may lead to a total system that is less than optimum.

So people who work on trees may be hurting the forest. This is hard to grasp, but the mathematicians can demonstrate it.

You should step back from your tree once in a while and try to get a glimpse of the forest. This is not easy. You get attached to your tree, and you are doing your best to make it the best tree ever. Even stepping back is dangerous because you might find that you were doing the wrong thing, or at least that your tree did not fit in very well with the rest. No matter how painful, you need to place your work into the larger context.

Life is a learning experience. The older you get, the less you know for sure. That is sometimes called wisdom. To know that you don't know has been called the beginning of wisdom. I believe that one aspect of wisdom comes from glimpsing the forest. Having the larger picture in mind can have great consequences on what you are doing.

Your boss is supposed to help you see part of the forest. If he is not doing that, bug him until he explains to you just what part your work plays in the grand design. What are you trying to accomplish in the larger sense and how is it to be done? The answers may be disquieting, but you have to know the answers before you can tend to your tree properly.

## Rule 101: Remember What You Are Trying to Do

It is easy to get lost in the maze and forget what you are supposed to be doing. This is because activity is sometimes mistaken for progress. So it is important that you take a sanity check every once in a while and try to focus on what you are trying to accomplish.

One of the great moral tales about this dilemma was told in "The Bridge on the River Kwai." In this film the British colonel, played by Alec Guinness, did a masterful job of pulling together his prisoner-of-war troops and building a great bridge. The problem was that the colonel got so wrapped up in building the bridge and doing a good job that he forgot that the bridge was valuable to his Japanese captors. The colonel forgot what he was supposed to be doing and helped the enemy instead of his own cause. This happens frequently in large organizations.

I once discussed a very big, expensive, and important project with a program manager. I had looked at his elaborate plans and concluded that they would work in a mechanical sense but would not accomplish the goal. In fact, I used the analogy of the "Bridge on the River Kwai" to illustrate my point. He got very mad at me. We parted company and, as far as I know, the well-constructed but ineffective program was implemented. So much for trying to be helpful!

My advice is to sit back from all of the activity once in a while and reflect on whether that activity is advancing the goals of the organization. It is possible in any large organization to keep busy without accomplishing anything. It is possible to attend meetings, write memos, take care of details, brief the boss, and make lots of telephone calls without having any useful result. It is possible to discuss and discuss and talk and talk without moving a bit closer to getting something done. You should be certain that this does not happen to you.

This applies particularly to government workers. Government is important. It is big. It is intrusive. Everyone wants less government, but there is great disagreement on which parts should be cut. Everyone seems to want to cut the other fellows' programs while still getting that lovely Treasury check in the mail for himself. This means that the influence of government in the lives, welfare, and security of Americans is not likely to diminish much in the next several years no matter which political party holds the presidency.

This being the case, it is necessary that the government actually sets out to accomplish what it is trying to do. The government should do work rather than merely create activity. There are some political theorists who assert that government should be inefficient and ineffective in order to lessen its impact on the people. I don't buy that. The goals and programs of government are established, indirectly, by the people, so government employees have an obligation to achieve those goals and carry out those programs efficiently and effectively. Efficiently in the sense of husbanding resources. Effectively in the sense of getting the job done.

Though the profit motive applies in the private sector, it is necessary to keep the objective in view there, too. Large organizations are vital to our economy and nation. They grow the food, make the products, provide the services, and handle the financing and communications that tie everything together. These organizations have to keep in mind what they are trying to do. When savings and loan companies forgot what they were supposed to be doing, disaster resulted for which we are all paying. When car manufacturers forgot what they were supposed to be doing, jobs were lost and families suffered. When corporate managers sacrifice long-term investment for short-term profits, international competitiveness is weakened. When large organizations forget their purposes, trouble happens.

Basically, the solution depends on the individual—government employee, corporate employee, institutional employee. If all of these workers band together to get the job done, things will be better. So my advice is to consider from time to time what you and your organization are trying to do and adjust your work accordingly.